GIVE A
F*CK,
ACTUALLY

GIVE A F*CK, ACTUALLY

Reclaim Yourself with the 5 Steps of
Radical Emotional Acceptance

ALEX WILLS, MD

Skyhorse Publishing

Skyhorse Publishing
Copyright © 2023 by Alex Wills, MD

First Skyhorse Publishing edition published 2023

Skyhorse Publishing books may be purchased in bulk at special discounts for sales promotion, corporate gifts, fund-raising, or educational purposes. Special editions can also be created to specifications. For details, contact the Special Sales Department, Skyhorse Publishing, 307 West 36th Street, 11th Floor, New York, NY 10018 or info@skyhorsepublishing.com.

Skyhorse® and Skyhorse Publishing® are registered trademarks of Skyhorse Publishing, Inc.®, a Delaware corporation.

Visit our website at www.skyhorsepublishing.com.

10 9 8 7 6 5 4 3 2 1

Library of Congress Cataloging-in-Publication Data is available on file.

Cover design by David Ter-Avanesyan

Print ISBN: 978-1-5107-7297-7
Ebook ISBN: 978-1-5107-7298-4

Printed in United States of America

Author's Note

Over the course of my clinical experience, I have been honored to witness my patients' initial discomfort, inevitable insight, and profound breakthroughs while practicing Radical Emotional Acceptance. The patients in *Give a Fuck, Actually* represent the many individuals who have bravely embarked on the path towards embracing their fucks. Central to my work as a psychiatrist is confidentiality. I took the Hippocratic oath to preserve the privacy of my patients. The composite characters in this book are entirely fictitious; any resemblance to actual persons, living or dead, is purely coincidental.

However, the emotions are very real. We all give a fuck, whether we like it or not. My hope, in creating these characters, is for you to find a piece of yourself. To embrace the unavoidable human experience of having strong emotions. As James Baldwin wrote: "It was books that taught me that the things that tormented me most were the very things that connected me with all the people who were alive or who had ever been alive."

Give a Fuck, Actually is as much a self-help guide as a collection of individual stories. While you will glean much emotional wisdom from meeting each character and practicing The Five Acceptances, they are not a substitute for therapy. This book is created to support, not replace, professional guidance.

For Mardi, who helped this deadened man begin to feel again

Contents

The 4th Acceptance

The 5th Acceptance

Appendix   **87**

Introduction

Ending the Vicious Cycle of Fuck Suppression

Have you ever wished we could cherry-pick what we give a fuck about? Wouldn't life be great if you could choose not to feel enraged, violated, betrayed, abandoned, fearful, vulnerable, or ashamed? If instead, you could skip straight to the good stuff and feel energized, happy, and grateful every single day?

And yet...

Despite all our clever fuck-denying mechanisms and fuck suppression regimens, we know the truth. We feel it in our sleepless nights and twisted guts. We do give a fuck, actually.

We're told *not* to give a fuck by everything from best-selling books to mainstream fashion. But contrary to popular opinion, that's impossible. The title of this book refers to the fact that we already care before we have any choice in the matter.

Emotional reactions (hereby called fucks) happen. No matter what, no matter how often we tell ourselves otherwise. Our fucks are no more under our control than robocalls at dinnertime.

As a therapist, I've seen too many patients who roll out yards of yellow police tape between themselves and their more vulnerable emotions. We view our emotions as something to be cordoned-off, over-intellectualized, minimized, or avoided at all costs.

In doing so, we compound our struggles. By denying our fucks, we create an exhausting battle within ourselves. Because not giving a fuck goes against our nature. It goes against our human hardwiring. And it goes against our quest for greater self-knowledge and actualization.

I've seen so much pernicious fuck blocking in my clinical practice, I coined a term for it: *emotiaphobia*: the irrational fear of emotions. *Emotiaphobia* is not to be confused with emetophobia, the irrational fear of vomiting. And yet, for both, the anticipation of puking or emoting can be worse than the pukefest or emotional outburst itself. It's the reason the fear of having a panic attack is often all that's required to bring on an actual attack.

We can trace all this avoidance to a single underlying fear: we will get stuck in a painful emotion forever. To avoid a permanent fuck-rut, we refuse to feel—not even for a moment. Instead, we tell ourselves: "I just don't give a fuck."

This adult lullaby works until it doesn't. By denying our human nature, we get trapped in a hellish loop of repetitive, intrusive thoughts, feelings, and bodily sensations. This is why our suppressed fucks can manifest as chronic stomach aches, sore necks, back pain, poor sleep, headaches, high blood pressure, hormonal changes, and even overactive bladders. Starting to sound familiar?

There's a better way. It begins with fully feeling each and every one of your fucks.

Yes, I'm afraid there's no way around it. I'm not a fuck-erasing wizard. But the process need only last a manner of minutes. From there, you can learn from the valuable emotional data your fucks provide and use that information to make better life decisions. After all, when you change your life for the better, you get new fucks. Better fucks. *Dom Pérignon* fucks.

This method involves dropping your defenses. It's not elaborate, expensive, or woo-woo. It doesn't require drugs, magic mushrooms, meditation, or any other altered states of consciousness. It only requires an attitude of acceptance for you to begin: acknowledging the fuck.

Fuck suppression is a vicious cycle. A trap we lay for ourselves, even with the best intentions.

Radical Emotional Acceptance is the way out.

Radical Emotional Acceptance

If you know anyone on the autism spectrum, or if you are on the spectrum yourself, I bet you're familiar with the concept of hypersensitivity. Of course, you don't have to be autistic to be a highly sensitive person, but for the purposes of this example I'm speaking to the extreme sensory sensitivity experienced by individuals on the spectrum. For example, a friend of mine was diagnosed with Asperger Syndrome at the age of three. These days he's a high-functioning logistician for a major shipping company, but once upon a time he was a grumpy-ass toddler who'd throw a fit if the tag on his OshKosh B'gosh overalls so much as riffled the small of his back.

My friend was so hypersensitive to clothing labels that his mom cut them out of all his school and gym uniforms. But that wasn't enough. The very texture of most clothing drove him crazy. He attended a parochial school that used a polyester blend for their uniforms. By the age of seven, he was the only kid at school wearing a homespun uniform of a white linen shirt tucked into drawstring pants; the bullies at school started calling him Lil' Amish Boy. The name stuck, and my friend's confidence cratered. Finally, his mom took him to a therapist for systematic desensitization therapy.

The therapist helped my friend get to the point where a formerly intolerable sound or texture became a neutral sensation. Over the course of treatment, what were once excruciating stimuli—halogen lights, the texture of raisins, a hug from daddy's steel-wool beard—became bearable, even a source of delight. Systematic desensitization therapy helped my friend recalibrate and become curious about these sensations: *How did the steel-wool texture make him feel? What were his natural responses telling him?* Eventually, a wool sweater ceased to be an iron maiden and started to feel like wool, like dad, like love.

Rather than avoiding the painful stimuli and compounding his phobias, my friend was gradually exposed to sensations that bothered him. At first, it was only for a matter of seconds, but he learned to abide his feelings of deep discomfort. Next, he learned how to get curious about those feelings. In time, he could tolerate his school uniform. After a few months of therapy, he took pleasure in wearing his poly-blend to school. No biggie, and no more Lil' Amish Boy.

Radical Emotional Acceptance, or REA, is systematic desensitization therapy for our fear of emotions. I have honed this approach with my patients over the past decade, and it delivers swift results. Instead of treating emotions as the enemy, they become our friends. Rather than avoiding our painful fucks, we feel them fully. We get curious. We start to explore. We become less reliant on our persistent thoughts, and more trusting of our sixth sense, that mysterious, gut-level instinct that guides us towards the light.

REA's psychological forebear is radical acceptance, a concept central to the emotionally-focused therapies which revolutionized my understanding of how emotions work. The core emotionally-focused psychotherapies informing The Five Acceptances—now get ready for the acronym parade—are Acceptance and Commitment Therapy (ACT), Dialectical Behavior Therapy (DBT), Dr. Sue Johnson's Emotionally Focused Couple Therapy (EFT), and Dr. Otto F. Kernberg's Transference-Focused Psychotherapy (TFP). My thinking on the intersection of mental health therapy and REA also owes a large debt of gratitude to Internal Family Systems (IFS), an integrative, evidence-based psychotherapy developed by Dr. Richard C. Schwartz.

REA takes these emotionally-focused modalities one step further. You can do more than grin and bear your discomforting fucks. To truly practice emotional acceptance, you must accept *all* of your emotions, both positive and painful. Affirming your joy is just as important as acknowledging your anger. Your fucks, in aggregate, give you insight into the desires, preferences, and values that form your sense of self.

As a busy doctor and a soon-to-be father of four, I've never found that mythical 25th hour in the day. But by accepting my emotions, I can tap into that honey pot of extra energy. I don't waste unnecessary emotional resources denying my fucks. When I feel overwhelmed or stressed—like I did, many times, while writing this book—I can cut through my need to "get it just right." I honor what's underneath: a genuine desire to improve people's lives. From practicing REA, I feel clear-headed, focused, and mobilized in ways I never thought possible.

In my clinical practice, I've seen how embracing fucks works as a powerful vaccine. It inoculates us from losing ourselves in toxic situations, because it keeps us honest— honest with ourselves. As soon as many of my patients learn to listen to their soul's calling, they find it impossible to remain in dynamics where they have to go against their own grain. REA, by definition, is an act of empowerment, not resignation.

Through Radical Emotional Acceptance, you will learn to trust your emotions. You will come to thank them for their service. Once you get the hang of it, you will find refuge within a maelstrom of fucks. Emotional literacy isn't taught in school, but it's something we must learn if we are to experience the deep rest that comes from making peace with our own internal weather. Believe me, you can go through years of advanced medical training without ever being taught how emotions work. Ever heard the saying, "Write the book you want to read?" For me, *Give a Fuck, Actually* is that book.

The Five Acceptances

The Five Acceptances are for everyone. They work anytime, anywhere, and are simple by design. Although they are presented sequentially in this book, you don't need to practice them all, or in any particular order, to get results. The Acceptances are like the stages of grief: denial, anger, bargaining, depression, and acceptance. It's more common to toggle back and forth between a few. Sometimes the Third Acceptance does the trick: Listen to the fuck. As you become a fuck-feeling connoisseur, you may find yourself exclusively practicing the Fifth Acceptance: Thank the fuck.

Give a Fuck, Actually is inspired by real patient encounters with Radical Emotional Acceptance. However, all characters you will meet in this book are fictitious composites informed by a decade of process notes and patient observation. I cannot overstate my gratitude for how my understanding and formulation of REA has been shaped by my patients, and the courage they have shown in meeting some of their fiercest emotions with an open heart. The creation of REA and the Five Acceptances has been an eye-opening journey every step of the way.

In the Preface, you'll encounter Tina, a rockabilly project manager who wants you to know she REALLY DOESN'T GIVE A FUCK that her best friend started drinking again. In Chapter 1, we meet Addie, who hides behind work, amphetamine salts, and merlot to deny her vulnerable emotions, with anger as her shield. In Chapter 2, we meet Daniel, a young movie buff who, in the midst of the Covid-19 shutdowns, has been deprived of his foremost fuck-denying mechanism: a trip to the movie theater.

In Chapter 3 we meet Mask Man (he also goes by Gabriel), who took a swing at an unmasked dude in Whole Foods in the pandemic summer of 2020. The altercation went viral (6 million views!), and now he must weather an international tweetstorm while trying to get a grasp on his short-fused temper. In Chapter 4, we learn of two sisters, Natalia and Emily, with similar relationship struggles, but vastly different outcomes. One sister married an overt narcissist, while the other sister married a covert narcissist. If you've never learned the distinction between the two, I hope this chapter is an eye-opener.

Each chapter is anchored by a single Acceptance, and a singular character's journey through REA. Chapter 5—the Fifth Acceptance—is the ultimate reward—the self-love that comes from radically embracing all our fucks.

Through the alchemy of acceptance, our sorrows and our joys become our teachers. Distress, when tolerated, turns into powerful insight. Yearning, when embraced, transforms into life-changing action.

So, are you ready to end your needless suffering and celebrate your fucks? Then let's begin.

The 1st Acceptance
Put Down Your Fuck Shield
Notice the go-to emotions you quickly turn to when you don't want to feel your deeper fucks.

The 2nd Acceptance
Name the Fuck
Observe all your fucks, big or small, and validate the reality of what you are feeling.

The 3rd Acceptance
Listen to the Fuck
Hear your fucks out. What do they have to tell you about your basic values and assumptions?

The 4th Acceptance
Act on the Fuck
With your newfound fuck wisdom, what choices can you make?

The 5th Acceptance
Thank the Fuck
Your fucks are your friends.

Preface

I Just Can't Stop It with the Fucks

From the moment she sank into my therapist's couch, I felt I'd seen Tina before. Was it the blunt bangs dyed Billie-Eilish green? The jumpsuit? The full-sleeve tattoos? My practice is located in downtown Boise, Idaho—the most geographically isolated capital city in the continental United States. If you're not in trail runners and a fleece jacket on a happy hour hike, you tend to stand out. I'd rearranged the furniture in my office the day before and my chair now sat at an angle with the patient couch. As Tina settled in, I saw the 25-year-old in profile: on her left bicep, the inked faces of Johnny Cash and June Carter gave me the once over. Beneath the country legends' portraits, a tatted scroll proclaimed *LOVE IS A BURNING THING.*

My first thought: Yes, it is. To be in love is to give a whole load of fucks. Second thought: Now I was sure I'd seen Tina's face before. A couple weekends ago, in fact, when my wife and I had one of my younger brothers over for dinner. After dessert, he scrolled through profile pictures on his dating app. "Nice ink," he'd said, handing his phone to my wife, in the way of a single guy seeking female validation of his dating choices. My wife murmured something diplomatic before passing me the phone.

I was certain the patient sitting across from me was the same woman my brother had swiped right on. The tattoo of country music's power couple was a dead give-away, but I also recalled her photo for another reason. In it, she wore a tank top whose stacked black letters spelled out I JUST REALLY DON'T GIVE A FUCK. In fact, there were multiple "reallys" sandwiched between the I JUST and the DON'T GIVE A FUCK.

"If it takes that many 'reallys' to insist you don't give a fuck, chances are you do," I said to my brother as I handed back his phone.

But Tina, in person, told a very different story than her Bumble profile. We were thirty minutes into our first session, and she hadn't yet named the subject that was, in her words, "not worth talking about."

"I don't even," she hiccuped, pulling out cowboy bandanas from deep inside her purse. I couldn't tell if she was about to cry or implode with anger. "I don't even know why I give a fuck!"

As a therapist, I get to experience the pantheon of people struggling to "simply" not give a fuck: to not give a fuck about their depression (rendering them even more depressed); to not give a fuck about their anxiety (as their thoughts spiral); to not give a fuck about their past trauma (as the nightmares intensify); to not give a fuck about their anger (until they finally explode). In other words, I see a lot of human beings.

"It's human nature to give a fuck," I said.

Tina gave me a once over in my office chair, and then scanned my framed medical diploma behind me. What did *I* possibly know about what it was like to be her? As she sized me up, Tom Petty's anthem, "You Don't Know How It Feels," played on loop inside my head.

My sense was that Tina was experiencing *shield emotions*. When our pain feels overwhelming, we reach for mental fortifications like apathy, anger, or nonchalance to obscure what lies beneath. Our emotional "shields" are usually stand-ins for emotions we have an even harder time accepting (say, feeling unloved or fearing abandonment), and no wonder even our shields can scare the living shit out of us. As I constantly remind my patients (shout out to Michael Brown's book, *The Presence Process*, for first introducing me to this wording): "Learning to work with our emotions is not about *feeling better*, but about *getting better at feeling*." Brown believes that whenever we feel discomfort, there is an opportunity for immense growth through learning the lessons of that moment—of all those painful fucks.

"Tina," I said. "Can you tell me more about this particular fuck?"

"If only it was just one fuck!" She pounded her hands against her thighs, a crumpled bandana squeezed in each fist. "I just can't stop it with the fucks! Over and over, I tell myself not to give a fuck. I say it to myself in the fucking mirror: Tina, do you give a fuck? Fuck, no, I do not give a single FUUUUCK! And I *was* feeling better. At least I thought it was working. But this past month—" Tina stared out my office window at the sunlit dome of Idaho's capital building—"this past month has opened up the fuck gates."

Opening up the Fuck Gates

Fuck gates, I thought. That's a good one. One of the many things I love about my job is that my patients are also my teachers. And yeah, we don't always speak the Queen's English.

"I'm hearing you say you felt pretty good for a while about not giving a fuck. Can you tell me what happened to open up, as you say, the fuck gates?"

"My best friend told me she was drinking again."

"Do you think she has a drinking problem?"

"Does someone who drives your kid sister to Jackpot when they're blind drunk have a drinking problem?" Tina snorted. "Does someone who gives you a cute dress for your birthday and then borrows it for a party where she pisses herself in front of your co-workers have a drinking problem?"

Her muscles were tense. On her arm, the lines around the Man in Black's eyes were deeply etched and unmoving. Despite her anger, she was hunched over in a posture of self-protection. Her face and the skin below her collarbone were flushed.

Tina, with her good-faith attempt to feel better, had declared war on herself. No wonder she'd found her way to my office. We needed to get to the *root emotions* Tina's righteous anger was covering up. I didn't know, exactly, what her preferred *fuck-denying mechanism* was—a behavior to stave off your fucks—but from what she told me, her best friend's numbing agent was Tanqueray and tonic.

"How did you feel, immediately in your body, when your friend told you she was drinking again?"

Underneath her seafoam green bangs, I glimpsed the dark arch of a raised eyebrow. She twisted her bandana, as if she was wringing out water. I waited.

"There are no right or wrong answers," I said. "The more honest we can be with ourselves, the easier it is to get in touch with our feelings. Becoming better at finding the valuable data our emotions provide—I call it *emotional data*—is the key to freedom."

I explained that our emotions are as nuanced as colors in the light spectrum. You can't pick and choose which colors to see or not see. You can't stand in front of Vincent van Gogh's "The Starry Night" and choose not to see the color blue. It's impossible. Or imagine waking up one morning and telling yourself that the color red is dead to you. Then you look out your window and see a big red stop sign. You'd be denying your own sense of reality.

But we do this all the time with our emotions, and then we wonder why we feel so defeated. Telling yourself you're going to stop an emotion that is already lodged in your amygdala and unleashing a complex chain of physiological reactions throughout your body is highly problematic. You can't help feeling what you feel. So, now not only are you experiencing powerful, embodied emotions, but your self-talk is telling you that your true feelings are somehow wrong. Now you're at war with yourself.

I tried again. "Your friend must have stopped drinking at some point for the news that she started drinking again to upset you. How did you feel when she quit?"

"Oh, that's easy," she said, releasing the bandana. "I felt proud of her. And most of all, relieved. When she drinks, her judgment goes out the window. For a year, I was scared to death she'd kill herself drinking and driving."

"Anything else?"

Tina sighed. "Now that I think about it, I was also exhausted. By that point, I'd staged three interventions, and I'm not a confrontational person. Talking to her directly about her behavior, and how it impacts all the people who love her—it took a lot out of me. She told me she was going to Refuge Recovery meetings. I thought she had a support group and was working hard to stay sober…"

Tina's voice trailed off. She was trying to make sense of her uncontrollable fucks. But the fucks kept coming, faster than she could tamp them down. Playing Whac-A-Mole with your emotions is a losing game.

"Okay." She took a deep breath. "You want the truth? Furious. Furious is how I felt when my friend told me she was drinking again. She'd only been sober for four months, maybe less." Despite her anger, Tina seemed to be losing steam. Her shoulders sagged.

"Furious, yes. That makes absolute sense. How could you *not* feel that way?"

"Maybe I overreacted," Tina continued. "But she made me so angry. I mean, I was trying to save her life. Or at least trying to keep her from fucking it up beyond recognition. But she didn't like my reaction. She claimed she'd gone back to drinking but was moderating and didn't need to go to meetings. Why was I making such a big deal about it? And then you know what she said? 'I'm so sorry I embarrassed you in front of your precious co-workers.' She said it dripping with sarcasm. More like a fuck you."

"It sounds like you've been deeply hurt by your friend's behavior when she drinks. Has she ever tried to make amends?"

Tina blinked. Her face hardened into the confrontational expression I remembered from her profile picture. "I didn't need an apology. I needed her to stop drinking. When she told me she'd gotten sober and was going to meetings, that was the only apology I needed."

"Are you sure that's all you needed? It sounds like you were really close friends, but she broke your trust."

Tina's shoulders began to heave. I could tell she'd been trying to suppress her fears concerning her friend's addiction for far too long, and she judged herself weak for still feeling them at all.

The Second Arrow Is Optional

This self-judgment—the self-talk that leads to further suffering—is what the Buddha called *the second arrow*. When we suffer a misfortune, two arrows fly toward us. The first arrow is the actual bad event. The second arrow is our reaction to the first arrow.

The first arrow hurts, but it is typically a discrete event. It's easy enough to examine and excise. The second arrow is the judgment (of yourself and others), the invalidation of your own emotions, the counterproductive self-talk, the intrusive thoughts, the hopeless wish to control someone else's behavior. When you prick yourself with dozens of daily secondary arrows, things get a hell of a lot more complicated.

In Tina's case, that first arrow is her friend's harmful behavior when she drinks alcohol. The second arrow is Tina's self-talk about her friend's drinking. Telling yourself you don't need to hear an apology from your friend when you really do? Second arrow. Telling yourself to just get over it? Second arrow. Telling yourself that you should read a book on how to *not* give a fuck, but even after you do, you *still* give a fuck—so what the fuck is wrong with you? Huge second arrow.

Secondary arrows suck, but they're suffering we bring upon ourselves. The good news is that second arrows are avoidable.

"When was the last time you spoke to her?"

"She's stopped talking to me. She won't return my texts or answer my calls. It's been three months. I know I was angry with her, but didn't I have a reason to be? I really give a fuck about her well-being. I, I—"

Tina was choking on her own truth. I see this a lot in my line of work. It's so hard for many of us to speak the deep truth of our own needs that we choke trying to get it out. Even so-called positive emotions can make us choke. Especially when we have gone down the rabbit hole of a toxic relationship, we may struggle to even name our most basic social needs. That's where our emotions come in: to remind us of our need for love and belonging.

"If you could tell her one more thing, if you could get her to listen—what would you say?"

"Please stop drinking. I love you. You really hurt me. Wait,"—she pressed a bandana to the corner of her eye and laughed ruefully—"that's more than one thing!"

"Exactly," I said. "That's a lot of fucks. No wonder you're exhausted." I looked Tina directly in the eyes. "It sounds to me like you lost your best friend. That sucks and it really hurts. It's a big fucking deal."

Tina squeezed her eyes shut. I stared at her green bangs, accepting whatever needed to arise. Soon I witnessed Tina's *shield emotions* of anger and resentment fall away. They were only confusing and obscuring the deeper, more vulnerable *root emotions* Tina had been feeling all along.

"I lost my best friend," Tina finally cried. "I don't know what more I can do about it and I feel helpless. There's so much hurt, so much water under the bridge." She looked up at me with clear wet eyes. "Where do I go from here?"

The 1ˢᵗ Acceptance
Put Down Your Fuck Shield
Notice the go-to emotions you quickly turn to when
you don't want to feel your deeper fucks.

Chapter I

Put Down Your Fuck Shield

It was five minutes before my last appointment of the day. I noted the feeling of tightness in my stomach. Why was I already feeling wary before the patient even entered the room? After a few months of working with this woman, I knew she suffered from severe childhood trauma that she was not ready to process. In her adult life, this trauma manifested as workaholism. In the evenings, she'd numb out before bed with multiple glasses of merlot. I also worried that another "-ism" compounded her struggles. I'd tried over many sessions to lead her through the process of Radical Emotional Acceptance, but I was beginning to suspect she only wanted one thing from me: her Adderall.

The stimulants allowed her to push herself even harder with a punishing work schedule. And the punishing work schedule excused her daily bottle of merlot. Two fuck-denying mechanisms all tied up in a sad little bow.

We all have fuck-denying mechanisms. But now I was beginning to see the writing on the wall. Because this patient refused to examine her patterns—in short, to change and grow—I began to feel the medication I prescribed for her was like putting a Band-Aid over a child's festering wound.

I'm a car and motorcycle guy—Evel Knievel, the stunt performer, cast a long shadow over my childhood in Twin Falls, Idaho. Six years before I was born, he attempted to jump the canyon in the center of my hometown on a steam-powered rocket. I'll put it this way: Adderall kept the engine running in her sporty little coupe while, with a glance toward the rearview mirror, she ignored the fire leaping from her back seat.

"Your staff is unprofessional," she said, when I opened the door to let her in. (My day was going hunky-dory. Thanks for asking.)

"How so?"

"I can't get my refills in time! Everything has been going great in my life. I've been super-productive—until a few days ago. That's when your office said it was too soon to refill my meds and I had to wait until this appointment. Now I've lost half a work week to feeling like shit. My depression is back. I can't keep up, and my anxiety is through the roof!"

I scanned the prescription database on my laptop. She'd requested her meds a week before her script ran out.

I told her how sorry I was for her distress and thanked her for her feedback. I also reminded her that she'd agreed to my office's medication policy, which clearly states we can't provide early narcotic refills without a consultation.

"I've been feeling so shitty I can barely get out of bed and you want me to call you!" she sighed, crossing her arms over her designer handbag. "This is your fault. You're holding my medication hostage!"

The tightness in my stomach became a painful throbbing. I felt a flash of white-hot anger. It jolted me to attention. I now realized I had a choice to make about whether it was beneficial to either me or this patient to continue our work together.

I am a licensed psychiatrist, but talk therapy is the most essential way I help my patients heal. Psychiatric medications are powerful, but I do not believe they should be the only tool in the therapeutic toolbox. Used alone, medications can be a blunt instrument. Most insurance companies will cover prescription medication, but many put limits on the number of counseling sessions or make it difficult to find an in-network therapist. This often leads to mental health issues being treated exclusively with medications that may temporarily reduce symptoms without getting to the root of the pain. In fact, prescription drugs can even become a roadblock to deeper healing by suppressing important emotional information.

Then there are the side effects. If you've ever gone to a doctor with a temporary struggle and been parked on antidepressants for years, you may know the hell of trying to wean yourself off decades of powerful neuro-chemical-modulating medications.

Without an understanding of our emotions and where they come from, a medication may cease to be an ally in healing.

Of Emotions and their Shields

A year into my professional psychotherapy training, I asked a Buddhist teacher, "Where are emotions located?" She looked at me funny, as if calculating the sincerity of my question. "Our emotions are in our bodies," she finally answered with a laugh. "Where else could they be?"

In conversation, we often use the words "feelings" and "emotions" interchangeably. There is an import-ant distinction. Emotions come from bodily reactions that are activated by neurotransmitters and hormones. Feelings are our conscious experience of those emotional reactions. For example, say you learn your friend just inherited an oceanfront mansion, and your rent is going up. Your shield emotions, envy and anger, might express itself as a fast heart rate, or a tightness in your chest. But in the moment, you might not even notice those physical changes. You're too busy feeling angry, which will man-ifest itself as thoughts, "Why is life so unfair?" or "Why do I have to struggle to make ends meet, while my friends live on easy street?" Our emotions are embodied, while our feelings are filtered through our mind.

To put it simply, emotions are the pure, raw, "feel it in your bones" truth. Feelings are heady and often obscured with automatic, negative thoughts that lead us to erroneous conclusions. If we focus just on our thoughts arising from our feelings—my life sucks; I can't catch a break; I should feel grateful for what I have; I'm a bad friend for feeling envious—then we miss the opportunity to become curious about our emotions, and explore the valuable *emotional data* underneath. Instead, we try to talk ourselves out of a bodily reaction that is out of our control.

The fact that our emotions are somatic is simple. But for some reason, this profound knowledge is not obvious to many of us body dwellers with human-sized brains. Take it from me: you can get through medical school and residency without ever understanding that emotions are physical. You can study the human body top to bottom— anatomy, physiology, pathology, pharmacology—and still wonder, "Where are emotions located?"

Our body contains infinite wisdom, if we choose to listen. But when we deny our fucks, we will be on the receiving end of the body-slam. Our deeper truths must cartwheel for our attention, kicking up bodily symptoms such as stomachaches, headaches, and changes in appetite.

That knot in your gut when you don't know how you're going to make rent next month? Embodied fear. The flush of heat to your face, chest, or pelvis when you're chewed out by your boss? Embodied shame.

Are your emotions having an inner tantrum? Then it's time to try the First Acceptance: *Put Down Your Fuck Shield.* The painful fucks you give in life typically start out as *shield emotions.* Before we can accept our fucks, we must become aware of how we unconsciously use *shield emotions* to conceal deeper, more vulnerable emotions, such as loss, pain, sadness, abandonment, and fear.

Feelings are emotions plus a story. Addie, my last patient of the day, was stuck deeply in her story—she was mad as hell (pure emotion) *and* it was everyone else's fault (emotion plus story). Her story could have fooled a lot of people with its righteous-sounding indignation, but it couldn't fool me. I knew the fiery emotion of anger fueling her aggressive narrative was a *shield emotion*— it covered up the deeper, painful emotions of sadness, fear, and despair she'd suppressed since her childhood abandonment.

How did I know she was experiencing a *shield emotion?* Well, my flash of white-hot anger was a *shield emotion*, too. *Shield emotions* beget *shield emotions.* When someone comes at you with their emotional dukes up, you tend to respond with your own defense mechanisms.

I first learned about these defensive, quick-on-the-draw emotions when I was leading an anger management therapy group at the VA Hospital during my medical residency in Hawaii. Despite the tropical climes, we presented the veterans with a drawing of the classic "Anger Iceberg." Imagine an iceberg: at the tip of the iceberg, anger is the most obvious and visible emotion.

But beneath the surface of all that frigid water we have other, more vulnerable emotions, such as fear, grief, and shame, needing to be felt.

Many of us are deathly afraid of what lurks at the bottom of our iceberg. We convince ourselves that our *shield emotions* are all that's there. We feel in touch with ourselves—"I'm just so pissed off!"—without pausing to explore what's underneath our fury. For others, anger may be too scary an emotion to access, so we swaddle ourselves in a cozy blanket of apathy, sanctimony, or "mild" disappointment—"I'm not angry, I swear!"—to protect ourselves and others from our anger.

All *shield emotions* start with discomfort. We feel the fuck. The fuck hurts. Because the fuck hurts, we quickly attempt to suppress the fuck with our preferred *fuck-denying mechanism*.

Some *fuck-denying mechanisms* are external behaviors, like drinking booze, popping pills, smoking a spliff, playing Call of Duty, watching Netflix, shopping online, doomscrolling, compulsive camping—you catch my drift. Other *fuck-denying mechanisms* are more internal, like intellectualization, rationalization, altruism, or humor. These cerebral behaviors are particularly sneaky, because our brains can convince ourselves we are doing the emotional labor by thinking through our feelings, without actually feeling them. Just about anything, when used to distract us from our emotions, can serve as a *fuck-denying mechanism*.

Judging ourselves for having a *fuck-denying mechanism* is not helpful. Sometimes, watching a unicorn cake get iced with buttercream on YouTube is exactly what you need to do after a hard day at the office. It's more about becoming curious about our emotions, and noticing the behaviors we often turn to for short-term relief.

But what are we actually afraid of? An emotion?

In short, we're afraid of being vulnerable. We're afraid of getting stuck in a discomforting emotion and it never going away. (This is impossible—particle physics-level impossible—but more on this later.)

In the depths of the Great Depression, President Franklin Delano Roosevelt said, "the only thing we have to fear is…fear itself." We fear feeling and accepting our fear. We fear our deep, more vulnerable emotions, so we throw up *shield emotions* in a futile effort to deny our fucks.

The Only Way to Stop Giving a Fuck Is to Feel the Fuck

I care deeply about my patients. Addie's wrath at the end of a long workday truly dinged me. To clear my head, I went for a stroll along the Boise River Greenbelt after work. I planned on doing a walking meditation under the cottonwood trees. I even brought my Tenkara fly rod along, just in case the trout were biting. And yet, despite the clear, calm, sun-dappled river—nature's Klonopin—my mind flooded with intrusive thoughts. My brain kept replaying the angriest parts of my exchange with Addie.

Phrases like, "You're holding my medication hostage" blared from my inner beatbox. And I responded, also in my own head, with what I wished I could have said to her accusations. If you're someone who worries you waste too much time playing on your phone, just think about how much time you spend having imaginary, fuck-giving conversations all alone in your own head.

As much as I preach the gospel of giving a fuck, I had to admit I'd unconsciously reached for my preferred form of *emotional bypassing*—a quick meditation—and, if I got lucky, a rainbow trout. Emotional bypassing is like trying to take a short cut through the field of your emotions. You try to skip over your discomforting emotions and go straight to your happy place.

Of course, the only way to stop giving a fuck is to feel the fuck in the first place. But I didn't want to experience my painful emotions. They fucking hurt. As soon as I realized what I was doing to myself—me, REA evangelist, attempting to deny my own fucks—I stopped walking. *Time to practice what you preach,* I thought. I found a bench facing the river and took a seat. With a deep breath, I practiced the First Acceptance: I put down my fuck shield. I admitted I was experiencing *shield emotions* to cover up my more vulnerable emotions.

The evidence in my body was overwhelming. When I tuned in to the subtle sensations, I could feel the knot in my stomach was still there. To top it off, I was feeling slightly nauseous and feverish—a common physical sensation when we feel we've been attacked, physically or verbally.

After fully experiencing the physical sensations in my body, I replayed the exchange with my patient, working hard to name each of my emotions.

The surface emotions I noticed were anger, frustration, and annoyance. All extremely common shield emotions. I felt these emotions fully, and then asked myself what deeper emotions the anger and frustration might be covering up?

The truth? Even though I had tried hard to help this patient, I felt a sense of failure. I was hurt by her criticism. It even stung, because our emotions are embodied as physical sensations. I felt sad because she didn't care to do the work of emotional introspection, even with my gentle steering. I was disappointed I couldn't do more for her, and acknowledged the likelihood that the only thing she wanted from me was a quick fix through medication. It's a tough pill to swallow that you can't choose the path of healing for others.

Addie had come to me for help and couldn't see how she was sabotaging her own efforts. But the fact is, she had come to me. My hard fucks came frontloaded with shame. I had failed to reach her despite all my therapeutic efforts. Therapists are commonly ghosted by hard-to-help patients—an unfortunate fact of the field that requires a large helping of REA.

Digging deeper, I noticed I even felt afraid. I feared this patient might leave negative feedback that could turn other patients away from receiving help, or cause trouble for my staff. I had no way of knowing what she would do next, and this made me feel vulnerable.

The deep emotions behind common shield emotions like anger and numbness? Typically, vulnerability and fear. Now, I'd hit bedrock.

Turn Your Fucks into Emotional Data

Just then, I experienced a remarkable shift. By consciously practicing the First Acceptance, the shift happened quickly—in less than three minutes. Now I once again felt compassion and sadness for this patient. After all, she was ignoring some heavy trauma.

I make it a practice of imagining that I *am* each patient. This is the only way I can come close to understanding their lived experience, without judgment, or projection. I closed my eyes and allowed myself to feel the depths of her wounds—the unresolved pain that fueled Addie's *"-isms"* and resistance to care. A terror so great, and so familiar, that denying its existence and bulldozing forward felt safer than allowing herself the space to heal.

Yes, my compassion was tinged with frustration for her victim mentality and disappointment in myself for not being able to show her a different way. I allowed myself a couple minutes to feel and validate these emotions, too. Our emotional landscapes are patchwork topography. More jagged mountains and hurricane-prone islands than a smooth fetch of water.

I'd come to the banks of the Boise River with the intention of meditating. If I'd begun my meditation before processing my own fucks, I would have spent the entire time growing increasingly agitated by my thoughts appearing in endless scroll, like the news ticker at the bottom of a TV screen. Ruminating and intrusive thoughts are useful indicators that we may be suppressing our emotions. These thoughts are most active when we are trying to "fix" our emotions rather than simply feeling them. Only after taking emotional inventory was I ready to begin.

I allowed myself to experience gratitude for all the fucks I felt in relation to this patient. My gratitude reminded me that I'm in touch with reality, in connection with other humans, and conflicts like this happen. And sure, I see tragedy in my practice in the form of wounded people who choose the pain that they know to the happiness they don't. I am also privileged to witness immense growth. Sometimes so swift it feels like magic.

Coming from this centered place, I acknowledged that there are times when it's healthier to end a relationship if the other person is not willing to change. I thought of Tina from the Preface, and how she had to ultimately disengage from her alcoholic friend. Tina felt she had done everything she could for her friend. She'd reached an impasse in the relationship where the best thing to do was step away.

Only when we have accepted our fucks and extracted all of our *emotional data* can we make the right decision. A personal decision informed by our truth is never wrong, because it's ours to make. By radically accepting my emotions, both the messy and the noble, I now experienced a flash of insight: I would work with this patient when she was ready. Until then, I would compassionately offer to transfer her medication to a different provider, leaving the door wide open for her if she decided to follow up with me. I made a note to myself to talk to my office manager about it in the morning and then stood up.

While I'd been meditating, the sky blushed to sunset fuchsia. I watched a gaggle of baby ducks gliding behind their mother. The goslings didn't have to paddle because they were being carried along by the river's current.

I smiled and thought, the fuck stops here. Not because I told myself to "not give a fuck." The fucks finally stopped because I noticed and accepted them as friends and teachers. By processing my fucks in real time, I was able to turn a painful situation into valuable *emotional data* in a matter of minutes. The kind of data that helps us make better life decisions.

I walked to the river's edge and loaded my rod, casting the line. The fly followed the snaking line, feather-like, dancing upon the swift current. Maybe my family would enjoy rainbow trout for dinner; maybe I'd return home empty-handed.

Either way, I'd return home a lighter, more peaceful person.

The 2ⁿᵈ Acceptance

Name the Fuck

Observe all your fucks, big or small, and validate the reality of what you are feeling.

Chapter 2

Name the Fuck

Daniel came in for his weekly appointment looking like he'd just had his ass handed to him. His face bore the signs of a sleepless night of crying, vomiting, or both. There were dark bags under his eyes. Burst capillaries like freckles speckled his eyelids. I took a deep breath and centered myself. Daniel, labelled bipolar by a previous doctor, had approached me for help with his mood swings. I could tell something major had happened, but we hadn't been working together long enough for me to guess the source of the many, many fucks he was feeling.

"Well, it's fine now." He crossed his arms defensively over his belly. "But we had a fight and Sarah, she kind of took off last night."

For a moment, I could feel his ache in my own stomach. "I'm so sorry. Can you tell me what happened?"

"I met a friend for a beer last night for three hours, tops. It wasn't even that good of an IPA." He laughed at his own joke, but his laughter fell flat.

I could tell he was trying hard to keep it together on my account. It's funny how many patients bottle things up or hide behind humor, even in front of their therapist. I get it. Too many of us, especially boys and men, are raised in a culture of flat-out denying our fucks. Many books for a male audience celebrate the "virtue" of "controlling" your emotions, which, in practice, leads to further self-alienation.

My own therapist pointed out to me several times, whenever I talked about emotionally painful things, I would smile or joke. Besides meditation, humor is my go-to *fuck-denying mechanism* to cover up my suppressed emotions. It was shocking to learn how un-self-aware I was of my own vulnerability. One thing I want to make perfectly plain as an Evel Knievel-loving Idaho guy: giving a fuck is far from emasculating. A man can feel strong—macho, even—in the midst of giving many fucks.

"When I came home, she had literally moved all her stuff out of our apartment. Well, I talked her down from it," he continued. "But her shit is still all loaded in her Saab like she might drive away at any second. She's parked on the north side of the street, and now that I think of it, it's Tuesday. Fuck! Tuesday is street cleaning. She's totally going to get a ticket."

Daniel let out a desperate growl, torn between picking up his phone to text Sarah and slapping it out of his own hand.

"Daniel." I pointed at the phone and clapped my hands. "Are you here with me? The person I want to hear from right now is you. Tell me exactly how it made you feel when Sarah packed up all her stuff."

"I know I shouldn't give a fuck anymore," he continued, squirming in his seat, "but I can't help it. That's pretty much my whole fucking problem!"

Daniel's fiancée, Sarah, had almost left him the night before and now he was feeling his fucks. This was perfectly healthy. The head-trip he was laying on himself for his inability to not give a fuck? Not healthy. Not productive. Second Arrow City. I would need to get him to stop shooting himself in the foot with his own compound bow.

During our first appointment, Daniel had told me that his bipolar disorder, what his family referred to as his "dark moods," was negatively impacting his relationship with Sarah. He said he wanted to learn how to better control his emotions. When I said to forget about control, Daniel shot me a look like, *Then, what the fuck am I paying you for?*

Small Fucks, Big Fucks, All Fucks

"We can't control our emotions," I told the bleary-eyed young man. "Observing our fucks and getting curious about how they make us feel is the path to sanity. There is no way around that. But it's possible to experience the fucks flowing through you in real time."

It bears repeating: we already do give a fuck before we have any choice in the matter. Fucks happen—no matter what, no matter how often we tell ourselves otherwise.

It was only our third session. I'd paid lip service to my fuck procedural before, introducing him to the First Acceptance, *Put Down Your Fuck Shield*. This is how I described it: Feel into your body to identify your *shield emotions*, like frustration, annoyance, or self-righteousness. Go deeper and ask yourself, what more vulnerable emotions are you hiding from?

But now, unbeknownst to the man whose hand was inching back toward the phone he'd slid under his messenger bag, he would learn the Second Acceptance: *Name the fuck*. We can't process our fucks without first admitting we have them. What are you feeling, actually? Stay with this fuck-feeling in order to accept your emotional reality.

Sounds straightforward, right? And yet most of us do the opposite. When we experience an emotion we consider negative, we tend to want to press fast forward. We often pull out our favorite *fuck-denying mechanism*.

I think I could guess how Daniel preferred to escape his fucks. It was early summer amid the coronavirus pandemic. In our last meeting, he suggested COVID-19 had ripped a hole in the fabric of his existence. No, he had said sheepishly, he didn't lose his job. He wasn't queuing at the food bank for a gallon of skim, or laying on a cot in a field hospital. Movie theaters were still closed.

"The last movie I saw on the big screen was *Parasite*," he'd said. "If someone told me that would be the last time I'd eat movie theater popcorn"—he stopped to shake his head—"I know I sound stupid. So many people have it worse."

In my practice, I do not discriminate against fucks, or compare one fuck to another. "Smalls fucks" and "big fucks" all deserve validation. Seemingly inconsequential upset, when examined without judgment, can reveal important *emotional data*. But more often than not, my patients come to me with what they deem small fucks, and then feel guilty for even feeling their feelings. What right do they have to complain, with a roof over their head and food on the table?

Even if you are the Queen of England, you are allowed to feel anger because your cat scratched a precious heirloom from King Henry VIII stored above your queenly bed. Minimizing your fuck, and shaming yourself for having a fuck in the first place, doesn't help anyone. In fact, it makes the fucks grow. It's fuck fertilizer. And we miss the important opportunity to understand what is beneath the fucks.

I noticed it was far easier for Daniel to complain about not going to the movie theater, than talk about his pain surrounding Sarah's departure. I suspected the two fucks were related. The more his relationship broke down, the more he needed an escape, and longed for his favorite *fuck-denying mechanism*.

I decided to use Daniel's *fuck-denying mechanism*, the movies, to guide him through the Second Acceptance, *Name the Fuck*. If I played my cards right, he'd be able to use this visualization exercise to go deeper into a painful experience, affirm his emotional reality, and leave his resistance behind. He could process his emotions, digest them, and move on. Like Metamucil for a constipated mind.

Accept the Reality of What You Are Feeling

When we're in the thick of an emotional struggle, it can be easier to accept our emotions if we imagine ourselves as a character. This does not mean replaying painful events over and over in your head, thinking of all the ways you could have acted differently. I also do not recommend this exercise for highly traumatic events. This can potentially be re-traumatizing, so please don't emotionally freeball unless you're supported by a trusted mental health professional. Observing your emotional reality through a visualization exercise is a deliberate, contained process to cut through your defenses and validate your *root emotions*.

"I want you to imagine the last twenty-four hours of your life as a movie," I proposed.

"What kind of movie?" Daniel sounded skeptical.

"One of the best movies you've ever seen. It probably has some happy parts, some sad parts, some adventurous parts, scary parts, and the movie itself is great in its entirety. The main character—that's you—will go through an epic struggle. We don't just love movies with happy endings where everything is wonderful and the good guy gets exactly what he wants in the end, right?"

Daniel nodded.

"What makes a great movie great," I continued, "is we get to experience a character process deep emotions. Because of difficult situations. Because of meaningful struggles. Would you even want to sit through a movie where the hero gives zero fucks?"

Daniel flipped through his mental IMDb.

"*Sahara,* 2015, with Matthew McConaughey," he shuddered. "I'll never get those two hours of my life back."

"Good, I can tell you're with me." I was about to guide Daniel through what could be a tough emotional reckoning. At least we had Matthew McConaughey alongside us in a Safari vest to lighten the mood. "Now, I want you to revisit the moment you knew something was up. Not from your perspective, but from the audience's perspective. Remember, there are millions of people watching you."

"Like in *The Truman Show*?"

"Yes!" I said. "All I'm doing here is encouraging you to live your reality from a new perspective. So, Sarah left you last night. It must have felt brutal."

"It was fucked up," Daniel took a shuddering breath and sank his head into his hands. "I mean, we had a fight the night before, but what couple doesn't fight when they've both been working from home in the same tiny apartment in the middle of a pandemic?"

"There you go," I said. "Your character already has a struggle nested within a struggle. He's living Steven Soderbergh's *Contagion*, and to top it off he and his fiancée are stuck in some bloodless version of *Panic Room*. It's impossible not to give a fuck for very long—at least through any healthy means. So, you walk through your front door. What details does the camera pick up?"

"Something was off. But it was subtle at first. I look around my living room and the first thing I notice is a poster missing from the wall." I could tell he was getting into it as he'd slipped into the present tense.

"Anything else?"

"Everything looks minimalist, and we're not minimalist." He let out a pained laugh. "I'm scared. My first thought is we've been robbed. I'm about to call out to Sarah, but then I notice all my music amps and pedalboards are still in the corner of the living room. That shit is cash money. What kind of a thief leaves the amps and steals a *Pulp Fiction* poster instead?

"What did you do next?"

"I call out to her. No response. That's when I go to the hallway and see the door to her home office is wide open. And there's nothing in there but power strips and dust bunnies. I mean, we're talking a room that was fully furnished and packed with her work equipment when I'd left the house three hours ago. She'd even been sitting at her desk, working! Now there's no chair, no computer, no fucking desk! She'd cleared the entire room. We're engaged. Who the fuck reacts that way to one fight?"

I had a hunch it wasn't just one fight. Although I don't know Sarah, I suspected she'd reacted from a place of past trauma. Too many fucks given and pushed aside before they can be fully processed is the typical source of knee-jerk emotional reactions.

"I can only imagine the gut punch of what you came home to last night. But the cameras are still rolling. Millions of people are feeling what you're feeling, and wondering what you're going to do next."

"I'm texting her, calling her, nothing. She won't pick up her phone. I'm sitting on our sofa under the blank wall where Uma Thurman used to be." He finally yanked a tissue out of the box next to him. "I'm so devastated but I also hate her for leaving no note or explanation."

"If that's the way she wants it," Daniel cried, "maybe I should have let her drive off. Would I even be feeling like total shit today if I had the strength to not give a fuck?" He shook his head. "You know what? I just don't. I don't even care." Daniel's chin began to quake.

Being at war with reality is really hard. Depleting. Exhausting. Futile. The good news? I could tell we were on the precipice of opening up those Fuck Gates.

Opening up the Fuck Gates for Emotional Data

"Daniel," I said, "Right now you're experiencing a part of your movie that's devastating. You give all the fucks in the world about Sarah, and you're feeling all those fucks. All those difficult emotions—grief, rejection, shock, hopelessness, uncertainty—whatever is in the mix, it's all part of your movie. Your feelings make sense. The audience is feeling them, too. And your movie isn't going to be great or powerful without this part. Can you tell me what happens next?"

"I hear her key in the door." He said it quietly. He was still decoding the meaning of the scene himself.

"The truth is, Sarah finally came home to me. Thank God she came home." Tears rolled down his face. "She said she sat in her car for hours trying to convince herself to drive all night to her sister's house in Vegas. But right when she had her keys in the ignition, she looked at the steering wheel of her car. And that's when she saw a ladybug."

"A ladybug?"

"Yeah, there's a ladybug in my movie," Daniel laughed through tears. "It was crawling along her steering wheel. She said it was like a messenger. When I was hospitalized a couple years ago—when I was first diagnosed as bipolar—Sarah went through hell and back with me. I went into a suicidal depression after what seemed like a manic period. But neither of us understood what was going on with me at the time. Not until my moods got so bad, I was a danger to Sarah and myself."

"It sounds like you've been through so much together."

"I scared the shit out of her with my mood swings," Daniel cried. "And now I've had some therapy to start getting my head on straight, but Sarah has never dealt with her own fucks. She told me last night how hard that period was for her. After seeing me in the hospital, when I was acting like a total shit head, she said she sat on a bench outside, trying to decide whether to leave me. That's when a ladybug landed on her knee. I mean, she'd been praying aloud: *Should I stay? Should I go?* She said the ladybug just looked at her, perfectly still. She thought it would fly off, but it stayed. She took it as a sign."

He squeezed his eyes shut. I could tell he was experiencing deep emotional pain as well as profound insight. In my experience, when you let yourself fully experience your fucks, you can learn from them as they flow through you. Since there's no such thing as controlling your fucks, isn't it better—dare I say, more efficient—to feel the fuck fully and move on, rather than get stuck in a fuck-denying cycle?

"When Sarah looked at her steering wheel last night and saw the ladybug . . . ." Daniel's voice trailed off. His fuck gates were now wide open; the fucks free flowing. This is often when we feel most vulnerable. "I dunno," he retreated, shaking his head and opening his eyes.

"I fucking love the shit out of that woman." Even as the tears ran down his face, I could tell his smile was genuine. "I don't know, Dr. Wills. Is our movie a romance, a tragedy, a comedy, or what?"

"All of the above, it's your show. Nobody knows exactly what it's like to feel those fucks except for you. Nobody can make a decision about what you need to do except for you. You're the only one with access to your emotions, so it's important not to deny them."

Daniel tilted his head, tipping back his tears.

"Emotions provide priceless information," I continued. "I call it *emotional data*. This data is what keeps us honest with ourselves and others. The emotions we try to avoid burrow deep, they worm into us. It's not the emotions themselves that are the problem. It's denying what you actually feel. These emotionally-suppressed worms—now you've got me talking bugs too—are what can cause someone to pack up her life on a Monday night in the middle of a pandemic."

"I think Sarah is starting to get that, too. We sat up all night talking. She told me our fight triggered her. All the stuff from a couple years ago came crashing back. Even though last night really hurt, she said she was proud of me for working on myself and she knew we'd been making progress as a couple. She even said she was going to make an appointment with a therapist. I'd almost forgotten she said that when I walked in here this morning. I think I was still in shock." He shook his head in wonder.

"She apologized to me last night. Said she was sorry she'd had this knee-jerk reaction. When she's scared she runs. She's realizing that's her pattern. She said it was like she was on auto-pilot until the ladybug snapped her out of it."

"I've noticed in my own life, sometimes things appear exactly where and when you need them to." I shared. "How are you feeling about your movie now?"

"I was in so much pain. Even a few minutes ago. It's not like the pain is all gone, but now it feels meaning-ful—I felt it fully and can see there was a reason. Last night was scary, but I learned that we have some work to do as a couple before we get married." Daniel looked me directly in the eye for the first time. "I think I'm even feeling gratitude that Sarah communicated something so important to me, even if her method fucking sucked."

"It sounds to me like you've accepted your emotional reality and, believe me," I laughed, "that's no small feat. Radical Emotional Acceptance of the present moment means you can acknowledge the present is shaped by a long chain of events in the past. We can't change the past, but we do have a choice in the present. Sometimes we're just too close to the action to see it. Being able to learn through a wider view of your own experience—a zoom out—is the whole purpose of the practice."

Daniel smiled. I had no idea what he was going to say next.

"I never thought about it before, but Matthew McConaughey used to star in a shit-ton of rom-coms." Daniel's energy had significantly shifted since he first entered my office. He had put away his phone and closed the flap on his messenger bag. He sat up straight like a man with a renewed sense of purpose.

"Even smug as hell McConaughey must have decided he had it in him to dig deeper."

The 3rd Acceptance

Listen to the Fuck

Hear your fucks out. What do they have to tell you about your basic values and assumptions?

Chapter 3

Listen to the Fuck

Dorothy Parker's name is synonymous with a quick wit. If the critic and satirist was alive now, she'd be Queen O'er the Tweets. And yet I can't buy into one of her most famous quips: "What fresh hell is this?" There are few fresh hells in life. Most hells are repetitive and of our own making.

Sometimes, Same Old Hell steps out in spit-shined Spanish leather boots, or a sequined dress you found in the back of your closet, but don't be fooled. Fresh Hell is usually Same Old Hell gussied up in disguise. We've just convinced ourselves each of our painful experiences is unlike any other. Thankfully, all it takes to start noticing our hell patterns is a little agency and introspection.

By practicing Radical Emotional Acceptance, we can name our fucks, and then learn from the valuable *emotional data* they provide. As our emotional literacy increases, and with it our ability to examine our emotions with an observer's detachment, we won't feel at the mercy of our inner weather.

We still feel all the feels, but with this newfound acceptance, we can begin to investigate our emotions for the kind of feedback that helps us make better life decisions. And making better choices is what leads to feelings of increased peace and satisfaction in our lives. This equilibrium can even feel like self-control. But the control doesn't come from ignoring our fucks—it stems from hearing them out.

This brings me to the Third Acceptance: *Listen to the Fuck.* Allow space for yourself to feel all of your emotions. Become curious about what those deeper, more vulnerable emotions can teach you.

Through the First Acceptance, *Put Down Your Fuck Shield*, we stood on the banks of our emotional current, still in our arm floaties. Through the Second Acceptance, *Name the Fuck*, we got a better look at what's in the current—not just the shallows, but also the deep eddies and whirlpools. Maybe we even dipped in our toes.

The Third Acceptance, *Listen to the Fuck*, is where we actually wade in the water and let ourselves drift. It's an exciting step.

When Core Beliefs Control the Current

Before we meet our next character, I'm going to briefly check in with Addie from the First Acceptance. She embodies an important concept: you can approach your problems from a place of victimhood, or from a place of *agency*. *Agency* is our capacity to exert power over our own experience. Victim mentality leads to further suffering, where personal *agency* gives us the strength to cope, change, and grow.

I don't want to pick on Addie. Yes, I was hurt by our encounter, but I used the First Acceptance (I put down my fuck shield) and Second Acceptance (I named my fucks) to quickly identify what I felt. I practiced the Third Acceptance by listening to what the fucks were telling me.

Time spent processing actual fucks? Two to three minutes. Only then did my fucks transform into actionable wisdom.

I mention Addie again to illustrate an important concept about *core beliefs*. Our core beliefs are often created during a period we have little control over—early childhood. They can be as life-affirming as *I am capable, I can deal with whatever life spitballs at me*, or *I am worthy of friendship and love*. We can also unconsciously carry forward destructive core beliefs from our childhood into our adult relationships.

But destructive core beliefs, when unexamined, can lead to a lifetime of unintentional self-sabotage.

Core beliefs such as *I'm not worthy, everyone I care about will eventually abandon me, nobody understands me,* or *I'm rejected when I seek help,* are tragically common. When it comes to my patients, most core beliefs boil down to three questions: *Am I valuable? Am I loveable? Am I worthy?* These are not trick questions. Any doubt about one's inherent worth, dignity, and right to a human existence destroys our sense of being unconditionally loved. The good news? All it takes to radically change your orientation to the world (and to even change how other people treat you) is a truthful exploration of your own core beliefs.

Only when we can finally identify our core beliefs can we change the beliefs that no longer serve us.

For example, a child who grows up with an abusive parent might develop the core belief *nobody understands me.* Afterall, this belief was helpful for a spell. Mom tearing into you when she's blackout drunk? Well, *she just doesn't get me.* Stepdad unwilling to accept your sexual orientation or even acknowledge you're gay? *Nobody understands me.* Or, even worse, *nobody wants anything to do with the real me. I must hide my true self to be accepted and loved.* Core beliefs are often formed in childhood as a protective shell, like the carapace on a snapping turtle.

Here's how Addie's unexamined core beliefs came back to bite her: This patient came to me because she felt anxious, depressed, and overwhelmed by her (largely self-imposed) workload. And yet, no matter how hard I tried, she resisted exploring her deepest, most vulnerable emotions.

All I could get from her was a Bob Ross painting of her childhood: a few dark pine trees here and there; a foreboding mountain. But I did learn that she'd been abandoned by her birth mother as a child and raised by her erratic, alcoholic grandmother. No wonder her bedrock core belief was *everyone will abandon me*. I might add to that, *because I'm truly alone in the world, I have to work really hard to make a lot of money in order to feel less vulnerable*. This patient was a self-avowed workaholic. For her, the amount of money in her savings accounts and stock portfolio was intimately intertwined with her feelings of personal safety.

So, what happens when a patient with a thick turtle shell and the core belief *everyone will abandon me* finds herself in therapy? My style is to follow the patient's lead and hold space for them to share their emotional reality—not to drag anything out of them. And yet, even my gentle approach was too much.

She retreated even deeper into her shell. She just wanted her meds. She just needed to work harder so she could feel in control. Why couldn't I understand that? Why was I encouraging her to examine her painful emotions? Why was I not okay with her escalating her use of amphetamine salts to keep up with her workload? Why was I against her?

The truth was, I was on her side. I wanted to help her, but she didn't want my help—at least not the kind I was offering. She just wanted her head meds, thank you very much, and in higher doses than I was willing to prescribe as she continued to ignore the root causes of her suffering. Her aggression and general lack of faith pushed me to the point of feeling like I didn't have any good options left. I referred her to a new provider, something I've only done a handful of times in my career.

Now she felt abandoned, and it was my fault for making her feel this way. After all, her core beliefs were unconsciously running the show. They were telling her the world is against her, everybody abandons her, even her doctor won't help her.

Who was the bad guy in her unexamined dynamic? Me, of course. According to her, nobody cares enough to understand her pain. And there I was, trying my darndest to understand! What was most important to me is that Addie begin to recognize the deep roots of her own suffering, to peel back her *shield emotions* to see the more vulnerable emotions that were running her show.

I led her to water, but I couldn't get her to drink. Because she was fixated on a quick chemical fix—on not giving a fuck and not gaining insight into her own relationship dynamics—she forced my hand. And so, I did the thing her unexamined core beliefs goaded me to do: I rejected her as a patient. Or, at least, this was her perception.

The only thing standing between Addie and a little peace was the Third Acceptance: *Listen to the fuck.* If she was willing to show some curiosity about getting to know and learning from her own emotions, she might have recognized how her core beliefs were hurting her relationships and causing her further rejection. Only when she acknowledged those dynamics could she have the power to let them go.

Change was in her hands. An end to the vicious cycle of abandonment was in her hands. Instead, she chose to stay in the hell she knew best. My rejection of her as a patient, as she perceived it, confirmed and strengthened her core belief: *everyone will abandon me.*

This is the essence of *confirmation bias*: the tendency to interpret new evidence as confirmation of one's existing beliefs and theories. Without curiosity toward and acceptance of *all* our emotions—especially those we deem too hot to touch—we're doomed to repeat our themes.

I invite you to take a moment to think of a difficult emotional experience you're currently dealing with; for example, feeling left out, taken advantage of, or undervalued—you name it. We all have our themes.

Now, as much as you can, take a bird's eye view of your life. Look for patterns in the landscape. Ask yourself,

When does this situation tend to repeat itself?
How might I be contributing to this Same Old Hell?
In what ways can I accept responsibility?

Sit with these questions and fully allow each feeling to bubble up. Drawing a complete blank? Good. Have the urge to throw this book across the room? Even better. Are you thinking—yes, these questions are fine and all, but my particular circumstance doesn't apply? Great. You're ready for the Third Acceptance.

It's not for the faint of heart. And that's okay. I know you're ready for it because you've come this far. I have faith in you as a person of courage. You've seen the river; you've traveled to the riverbank and looked hard at what roils your waters.

Now it's time to swim with the current.

Mask Man, Unmasked

Gabriel sank into my couch like it was a baseball dugout and went into a huddle. He had come to me six months earlier, wanting help with managing his anger. Ionization fans whirred around us, neutralizing airborne microbes. This was before COVID-19 cases had spiked in Boise, and my office began requiring both therapists and patients to wear masks in session.

"I'm sure you saw," he mumbled, face in his hands, the purple dome of his Boise Hawks ballcap his only protection. "The clip doesn't show the whole story."

He looked up at me. I wasn't following.

"The viral video? Six million views?" He took off his cap and ruffled his matted hair as he looked me in the eyes. I still wasn't tracking. "At Whole Foods? I'm the guy they're calling 'Mask Man.' Any of this ring a bell?"

"Woah, that was you!" I'll admit this wasn't exactly a therapeutic response. A patient achieving national infamy from a trip to the grocery store was new territory for me.

It was the summer of 2020, and a senseless culture war was brewing over face coverings to slow the spread of the coronavirus. It seemed like anyone, at any moment, could be caught in its crosshairs.

"I went out a couple nights ago to pick up some vitamins for my son," he began. "I'm standing in front of the shelf where they have the Emergen-C. I'm all masked up, I'm wearing gloves, I'm trying to be super careful. And just when I'm crouching to read the label on a bottle of vitamins, this big bearded dude crouches down next to me. He's literally twelve inches away from my face, no mask, breathing on me. And he's not just any breather. He's one of those mouth breathers."

As I imagined myself in Mask Man's situation, I couldn't help but feel the urge to clock the guy, too. "It's not as simple as you came up to the guy and took a swing at him, right?" I asked. That was the part of the clip playing on multiple cable news channels. "Lucky for you, you missed."

Mask Man nodded vigorously. "Coulda been even worse, I know. The guy chose not to press any charges." He shoved the ballcap back onto his unkempt head. I could tell he was feeling particularly vulnerable. Not just from the media attention, but from my probing.

"I've barely slept since it happened. This morning I was breathing into my kid's paper lunch bag to keep from hyperventilating."

Since Mask Man had started therapy to investigate what was under his short-fused rage, there had been no major breakthroughs. Because he was consciously aware of his anger management issues, he had a lot going for him. I saw him as a patient with great potential for growth, but only if he was willing to explore what his go-to *shield emotion* was covering up.

"You have to help me get control of my emotions," he had pleaded during our first appointment.

"What if I told you there's nothing to control?" I said. It was not the first time I had said this to a patient.

"Sounds like some Zen-level shit." I assured him you don't have to be a monk to believe it. Through a decade of clinical experience, I've learned what spiritual teachers have insisted across millennia: we can't manipulate our emotions.

"This pandemic is bullshit," Mask Man continued. "I don't mean it's a hoax. It's very real, but the way it's making people act? It's driven all the shitheads out from the woodwork. Have you heard about the alleged 'Face Mask Exemption Cards' people are carrying?" He put up his fingers in air quotes.

I needed to get Mask Man back on track. If he was one of those Sartre-sympathizers who believes hell is other people, I would gently point out, *You are a person, too.*

For our first month of talk therapy we'd concentrated on the First Acceptance: Put Down Your Fuck Shield. In his case, his main shield emotion came in the form of a left hook. During our last appointment, he was starting to see that his "anger management issues" might be covering up something else. Often, our raw emotions are so deeply rooted and safely protected, it takes work to even name them. He would have to look at why he kept pinging Same

Old Hell, and what negative core beliefs were running the show.

"I've heard about the fake medical cards," I said. "And I saw you take a swing at the guy on the news. Can you take me back and tell me what happened before things escalated? Try your best to use emotion words to describe what you were feeling."

"Well, like I said, Mouth Breather was right beside me, super-spreading his droplets everywhere. Wearing no mask and it's the store policy to wear a mask while shopping. They even give you a mask if you don't have one. Why did this guy think he was the exception?"

"I understand. I'm hearing what he did, and what you thought. But how did you feel?"

"Pissed off. Why should I be the one who had to leave the aisle? I'm following the rules and looking out for my fellow man and this guy has the nerve—" he paused, running out of breath. "I had no choice but to sock it to him."

I paused, waiting for him to continue. Mask Man furrowed his brow. "Well," he paused. "when I think about it now, maybe I could have ordered some sliced turkey from the deli and gone back to the vitamin aisle when he was no longer there. But still—it's more a matter of principal."

"They do have good deli meat," I said. "The guy may have moved on and you would have probably felt a lot safer. Did you have any idea why he wasn't wearing a mask?"

Mask Man's breathing slowed down for a second as he tried to think. "His excuse doesn't matter. I told him he was endangering all the other shoppers." He blinked. "I guess I could have asked a store clerk to talk to him. It's the store's rule, after all. He was just making me so fucking mad . . . I couldn't think clearly in the heat of the moment," he mumbled.

"Tell me how it felt to be you, in your body, at that particular moment."

"I felt this terrible rage inside. Like all the blood in my head went from lukewarm to boiling hot in a second. I'm thinking, *selfish people like him are going to be the death of us all.* And that's when I told him he should be wearing a mask."

"How did he respond?"

"He glanced at me out of the corner of his eye—he was a big guy, in pretty rough shape—and took another big wheezing breath through his beard. He was crouching to read the label on a bottle of vitamins. He went back to reading the label and then he said something to me, pretty much under his breath, but I heard him loud and clear."

"What did he say?"

"*You sure look different than the last time I saw you, Ma.*"

I laughed. I couldn't help it. "That's kind of funny," I said. "And I see how he got a rise out of you."

"People have lost their jobs, they can't make rent, can't make car payments, can't make plans for shit. If you're lucky to still have a job and can't work remotely you're worrying about bringing the virus home to your family.

Everyone's raw, you know? That short fuse is real—" Mask Man continued, retreating behind his *shield emotions*, this time in the form of an angry diatribe.

Shield emotions are the feelings we put up to block or avoid—dare I say "mask"—other emotions. As a general rule, if you're experiencing self-righteous thoughts or brain-driven rationalizations, there's a good chance your subconscious has created a shield between yourself and your deeper, too-hot-to-touch feelings.

"You keep saying 'everyone.' That 'everyone' is stressed. That 'everyone's' nerves are raw. Is this one guy without a mask in the vitamin aisle an exception?"

Mask Man paused. His hands were coiled in tight fists. He began nervously bouncing them against his knee-caps. "I was just so fucking angry," he said breathlessly. "I took out my wallet and let the billfold drop. I pretty much thrust it in front of his face—I guess that was pretty aggressive—and said, 'See that little boy? That's my son. He's eleven years old and he's immunodeficient. And when I see people like you not wearing a mask'"—I noticed his hands beginning to shake—"when I see people like you, I think, *he's as good as dead*." With this he lowered his head into his hands once more and took a deep shuddering breath.

"I feel like I can't breathe," he said, waving his hand at me to look away. "It feels like a hot rock is crushing my chest . . . I can't fucking take one more second of this." Now his whole body was shaking. Mask Man was crying. I'd never seen him cry before.

"I know these feelings are really intense," I said. "If you can, try to consciously slow down your breathing. Would you believe me if I said you're making major progress right now?"

"What?" He angled his body away from me on the couch and was attempting to brush away his tears with the back of his hands. He was one of those guys who won't even let his therapist see him cry.

"Your *shield emotions* are very real. And they're nothing to be ashamed of. They have a purpose, and they're not the enemy. Even your anger and rage—they're trying to teach you a better way. Your *emotional data* exist to help you make better decisions in life—as long as you're willing to listen," I said. "The Third Acceptance, *Listen to the Fuck,* is not always easy to follow. We're used to listening to the noise of our thoughts, not our emotions."

"Why? Why am I so fucking angry? It's been my default emotion my whole life. I mean my childhood was pretty normal, I just feel so—" His voice trailed off in exasperation.

"That's a high-intensity, exhausting way to live. And you rarely let anyone see this side of yourself—the more vulnerable parts. From a therapist's perspective, it's like I'm trying to look under the hood of a fire-spitting hot rod." I knew Mask Man was into cars. "This is the first time you've let me look under the hood. Can you tell me what's underneath?"

"Fear." He practically wailed it. "There's so much fear. I feel scared for my son. He's so vulnerable and it makes me feel vulnerable. If I brought this virus home to him and he got sick"—now the dude was straight up sobbing—"If I brought this thing home to him I could never forgive myself. I was just trying to buy some supplements for my son to get him through this, to feel some semblance of control. And then Mouth Breather had to go and . . . FUCK!" He let out a low, rattling cry.

We both sat there in silence, unmoving. "Where does the fear come from?" I asked carefully.

"I dunno," he mumbled.

I waited.

"I guess I've always felt like I have to be on my guard all the time around other people, even before the pandemic," he said quietly. He looked up at me, as if asking permission to continue—"because the world isn't safe."

Mask Man had just spoken a core belief. He had to protect himself, because the world wasn't safe. He couldn't rely on anyone else. How, exactly, he had come to learn this negative core belief, we would get to later. That would take more trust, and more sessions. But first, I needed to validate his reaction to the underlying narrative that was running his show.

"Yes," I said. "It makes so much sense why you feel so angry. Why you're quick to throw a punch. If there is a voice, deep inside of you, telling yourself that the world isn't safe, no wonder you're often on the offensive. No wonder other people feel like the enemy. How could you trust them to protect you, if your own core beliefs are whispering to you, over and over, *the world isn't safe*."

Mask Man bobbed his head down just a little, in agreement. His bottom lip stuck out, his face contorting every so slightly. I could tell I was beginning to meet the sweet, scared young child that lived inside this grown man's frame.

There was a long stretch of silence. "I was just so angry. Another customer yelled at me to chill out, and that's when I snapped: I turned to the guy and aimed for his face. I was on autopilot at that point. The woman who yelled at me to chill must have started recording us on her phone," he continued. "So did I do bad? Did I do good? Twitter's kind of split on the subject of me, now that I think of it. Am I a health crusader? A world-class asshole? We've been working on my issues for months. I should have been more skillful in the moment."

Emotions Are Our Teachers

"Look, this moment feels overwhelming because it is. The future is unknown. Your immunodeficient son is vulnerable. And there's so much outrage going around. There'll be a replacement hero, or villian, trending by six o'clock. But here's the hopeful part: your emotions are telling you your deep truth. And your truth is what puts you back in the driver's seat. And by 'emotions' I'm not only talking about the *shield emotions* that made you take a swing at the guy, but the deep-down stuff," I added.

"You mean the fear." Gabriel looked up at me with tired eyes. "The fear under the hood."

"Yes!" I said. "Fear. You felt a shit-ton of fear! There is nothing wrong with that. Your *emotional data* made you aware of a threat. Your emotions were helping you. They were trying to protect you from a real threat. Well, they were helping you until you blew your own fuse."

Mask Man stopped to contemplate what I'd just said. "The guy was probably picking up on my fear, right? His coping mechanism was humor, but he had a tough audience in me. And the customer who taped it all? Probably fearful, too. Fear is as contagious as any virus, isn't it?" He paused, glancing up at the ceiling. "Oh my god!" His face flushed with remorse. "I was the super-spreader!"

"What if I told you your fear serves a purpose?"

"Even if it made me explode with anger?"

"Was it the fear that made you explode or was there something more to it?"

Gabriel glanced out the window. "I guess I felt like I had no options," he sighed. "I mean, I can think of a couple now, but not that night"—he shook his head—"Jesus, I really do go into full-on roid rage when I feel threatened! If I'd just been able to take a step back and practice that REA thing in the moment—none of this had to happen."

"It had to happen because it did. Your emotions are teaching you something. You're learning that your fear and vulnerability manifest as rage. This is valuable *emotional data*. Data you can use immediately to make better life decisions. Now you have options, now you have *agency*. You can choose to radically accept the temporary but intense emotions of feeling overwhelmed."

"Accept feeling overwhelmed?" Gabriel asked, incredulous. I'd noticed his energy shift the moment I said the word.

"How do you think your evening might have gone if you'd accepted that you were feeling overwhelmed? That you were on a short fuse and needed to de-escalate your interactions with others?"

"I guess I could have used one of those grocery delivery apps, or made another meal of pantry-pasta and put off going until tomorrow. At the very least, I could have avoided the guy," Gabriel hung his head. "Or tried to have a real conversation with him."

I nodded. "But could you have listened? You were too caught up in anger—in your most effective shield emotion—to even hear yourself."

"I've been fuck-blocking myself for a long time, haven't I?"

The 4ᵗʰ Acceptance
Act on the Fuck
With your newfound fuck wisdom, what choices can you make?

Chapter 4

Act on the Fuck

Through Radical Emotional Acceptance, we're able to acknowledge and explore our hard knock fucks because we know they are temporary. As my friend's Texas grandmother used to say, "the worm will turn." I have no idea what that means, but I like the sound of it. What I do know is that as sure as the worm will turn, the fuck will pass.

Just like your fucks, this chapter serves a specific purpose to remind you that fucks are fleeting. However, it comes with a trigger warning, as this story includes multiple profound, but unflinching emotional truths.

In "A Tale of Two Sisters," I offer two paths drawn from a decade of clinical experience. There is no double-blind study for comparing outcomes between those who work against their fucks and those who work with them.

Instead, I present Natalia and Emily, raised by the same parents, with similar vagaries of nature and nurture, and similar relationship struggles.

Although these sisters are composites, their toxic emotional education as children led them to struggle with emotional literacy as adults—a background many of us share. One sister chose to suppress her fucks while the other sister eventually chose to accept her fucks. Despite their struggles, each sister had the power of choice. This is the essence of Acceptance Four: *Act on the Fuck*. The wisdom of our emotional data empowers us to make the best choices for ourselves.

In our last story, one sister deals with her struggle and strife by telling herself, "I just don't give a fuck." The other sister learns to practice Radical Emotional Acceptance and find *agency*—not right off the bat, but after many false starts and much pernicious fuck-blocking.

Now let's see how fuck acceptance versus fuck suppression played out for Natalia and Emily.

A Tale of Two Sisters

10:59 a.m. on a Thursday. I prepared to watch the minute hand on my desk clock crawl from 11 a.m. to quarter after. My weekly dose of watching paint dry. In all our time working together, Natalia had never been on time. She had her reasons, many of which made me worry about her home life, but we'd come to a truce that late was better than never. When the office manager buzzed me on the hour to say Natalia was ready to see me, I felt a twinge of hope for her predicament.

"I got my own wheels!" Natalia said breathlessly as she entered my office, clutching a key fob in her hand. Natalia, in addition to two sons of her own, had also been raising her niece for the past nine years. The niece was the daughter of her sister, who was down on her luck in ways Natalia insisted she wasn't ready to talk about. "My sister is off limits," she'd warned me during our first meeting. I assumed her sister was in the grips of long-term addiction, but Natalia had so far refused to offer me so much as a corn nut of context. I felt confident her sister's story would only come to light after Natalia had accepted her own emotional reality.

Although she was only 39, Natalia often looked older than her years from decades of slow-drip emotional abuse at the hands of a passive-aggressive narcissist husband. I'm hesitant to label a person I've never met as a narcissist—after all, we can all display some degree of narcissistic behavior when we are under stress, on drugs, or otherwise not at our best. But I had a clear sense of him, based on what Natalia had told me in previous sessions.

I pictured Natalia's husband as a Narcissist with a capital "N": one of the overt types who never stop talking about themselves, cannot empathize with their loved ones' struggles or celebrate their achievements, and have a tendency to suck all the oxygen out of any room they enter.

"That's immense!" I said. "How'd you pull off getting your own car?"

"I thought I had no assets—Rob controls everything. Even our family car is in his name. But then I thought of all the old cowboy tack I'd inherited from my grandfather. It was just sitting in the storage unit, so I made some moves while Rob's been out of town on business. I called an auction house and paid a couple movers to take it over to them in one haul. I never thought it would be worth much, but I knew it was worth something. Rob would say things like, 'What are you going to do with a bunch of riding tack and ol' coyote traps and a jar of rattlesnake tails? Maybe it's your granddad's way of saying you're not worth a hill of beans—all the way from the afterlife.' Turns out all those Western saddles were worth around 3K at auction. Enough to buy my friend's old truck in cash. She just signed the title over to me this morning."

Natalia laughed easily as she told me of her triumph. I realized I'd never heard her genuine laugh before. I was used to the hard, nervous titter she passed off as a laugh. As I turned over the pages in her file, I felt overcome by a sense of wonder at the transformation. Here is a smattering of notes from one of our previous sessions:

I've been carrying the weight of this my whole adult life . . . I'm just ruined. My body is in so much pain right now. Rob took the truck, held us hostage again, had to borrow a car to get here. He's overwhelmed. Been more so since he's had to provide for my niece. I've been sitting at home in fight or flight the whole time he's gone. It's just another tactic. . . I'll break down, end up in a psych ward. He's setting me up to freak out and I'm trying so hard to stay grounded. I know I can't change him, I can't fix him, but it is so . . . I'm not crazy, right? But we have a home life and it's beautiful, we want this so much...

Deep and powerful truths. So powerful, in fact, I felt fearful for Natalia again as I skimmed my notes. She swore her husband had never physically abused her, but he'd been emotionally abusing and manipulating her since a young age. They were high school sweethearts. I'd been doubling down on teaching her Radical Emotional Acceptance as a way to see her straitjacket marriage clearly: for what it is and not what she wishes it would be.

Despite her husband's domineering disposition, Natalia was insistent in her devotion—until today.

If you've never been in an abusive relationship, you may have a hard time wrapping your head around how someone could say, "We have a home life and it's beautiful," and "Rob took the truck, held us hostage again," in the same breath. And yet, if you've had the experience of being in love with an abuser, you're probably shaking your head in painful recognition. Love is not logical. People with codependent tendencies—Natalia had them in spades—are simply more susceptible to abusive relationships with narcissists.

Codependency, most simply, is an extreme form of people-pleasing. It was first used in reference to the partners of alcoholics, but has come to include any relationship dynamic where someone takes full responsibility for meeting someone else's needs, thereby denying their own.

I believe that practicing Radical Emotional Acceptance is the antidote to unhealthy, codependent relationships. As soon as my patients begin to honor their own fucks, it becomes impossible for them to lose themselves and go along with their abusers' twisted definition of "love."

Radical Emotional Acceptance doesn't mean staying in a toxic situation. What it does mean is fully acknowledging and accepting our deep emotional truths in order to inform our decision making. Our fucks serve a purpose. Our fucks guide us towards wise choices. Cue the Fourth Acceptance: *Act on the Fuck.*

It's important to note that not all fucks are painful. We give a fuck about what we like, love, and desire. We give a fuck about what we care deeply about. We all draw on a vast repertoire of positive fucks.

What deep emotional truths had Natalia come to accept since our last session? How, after so many years, had she begun to validate her own desires and preferences?

Her own joyful fucks?

I asked her—I sincerely needed to know: What had spurred this remarkable turnaround?

"It was the final straw," Natalia said. "Not the biggest straw, that's for sure, but the last one. I have a little left over from the auction to start a cash stash. I'm beginning to plan my exit strategy. Not just for me, for the kids. I'm terrified Rob will find a way to take everything."

Her eyes shone as she fiddled with the new key fob in her hand. She actually looked physically younger today. More 30 than 40. But I still didn't understand what Natalia's final straw had been.

"Long story short," she began. "Our oldest Jason just graduated high school and I wanted to throw a party. His graduation was cancelled because of the coronavirus, so I made an extra effort to get a few family members and friends together. We kept it small—ten people—but I asked everyone to bring a favorite memory of him to share. It could be a photograph, a story—his best friend even made a mix tape of their favorite songs. Everyone came through with something. Well, almost everyone."

"Let me guess, Rob did nothing."

"Worse than nothing. He was busy sabotaging the party while I ran interference. The day was supposed to be about Jason. You only graduate high school once." At this, Natalia squeezed her eyes closed. When she opened them, they were wet with tears. "Just when the toasts began, Rob went into the hallway and began talking loudly to Jason's best friend's new girlfriend. I get why she's standing in the hallway, she's the only guest that doesn't know us well. The dining room was crowded. But for my husband, in the middle of his firstborn son's graduation party, to join her and start going on about politics? His voice was so loud, no one could hear the favorite memories. All eyes should have been on Jason."

"He didn't stop?"

"You bet," Natalia answered, the light in her eyes intensifying. "He kept it up until the last couple toasts, when my friend finally said something. I sure as heck didn't say anything. He would have steamrolled me."

"You realize that's textbook passive-aggressive narcissistic behavior, right?"

"You bet," she said again. "You bet" is Idahoan for affirmative.

"Do you mind if I read you something you said to me during one of our last sessions?"

Natalia's eyes widened, but she nodded her agreement. I didn't think it would be easy for her to hear her own words from only a couple weeks back, but I could tell she was feeling strong. Unusually so. There had been a major change in her—an "aha" moment.

"As you're listening, think about what's shifted over the past two weeks. Here goes:"

My husband shut down his feelings when he was 14 and never learned how to grow. He's proven to me over and over again he will not get help. When I ask him to stop, he says, "you're right, you're right, I get it." He is not a monster. But he keeps acting like it's my fault—because I annoy him, you know? I go off on him, and then he goes Jekyll and Hyde. It's like I ask him to abuse me . . .

Natalia shook her head as I read her words back to her. She cringed when I repeated the last line.

"I said 'I ask him to abuse me?' That sounds like Rob talking, not me."

"Yes, in codependent relationships, it's easy to become so enmeshed, you lose sense of your own voice, you start doubting your *sixth sense*. You become merged with him. And his manipulative logic gets mixed up with your valid observations. Adult narcissists are wounded children inside, but it doesn't excuse their behavior. Rob acts like his own kid is competition, and refuses to get help. Yet you found the strength to reach out for help on your own. From what you've told me, he's been gaslighting you since you were teenagers. He makes you feel crazy by constantly invalidating what you know to be true. With gaslighters, up is down; the sky isn't blue, it's whatever color they say it is and you need the eye exam, right? I've seen what decades of this kind of insidious abuse can do to people. That you could clear your head, even for a few days, of Rob's controlling voice, and buy you own car and start planning a better life for you and your kids—"

"Insidious abuse?" Natalia interrupted. "You're calling what Rob does insidious?"

I thought I was on a roll. But I've been a therapist long enough to pay close attention when a patient clings to a single word from a larger observation.

"Yes. Not like a horror movie. Insidious as in, having a gradual and cumulative effect."

She closed her eyes and took a deep, sucking breath, like a swimmer's last gasp of oxygen before plunging under the water. I watched in bewilderment as she drew her knees up into her chest on the couch.

She let her head drop between her legs. Now she was tucked into herself, curled up tight as a dead millipede. What in the world had I said?

"His abuse isn't insidious." She said it so quietly, with her face wedged between her knees, that I had to ask her to repeat herself.

"I said, his abuse isn't insidious! I would never call it that. I would call it pretty fucking obvious." There was a sudden edge of anger to her voice. "But I'm the codependent, right? I have difficulty making decisions in a relationship, difficulty communicating, difficulty even describing my basic feelings. Therapy"—she shook her head—"It's like I've opened up my own can of worms. So yeah, I know I'm codependent—I know I've let him control and manipulate me—but since we started talking, I can finally recognize my truth. You know how I know when it's a deep truth?"

"How?" I said gently.

"As soon as I started accepting my emotions, I started noticing everything. I mean everything. It's like you popped out from under some freeway underpass and squeegeed my windshield. Now I can see clearly. And what I see fucking hurts."

"Yes, it should hurt, because it does. You should feel exactly as you feel, because you do."

Natalia let out a low moan. I could tell she was feeling extremely uncomfortable. Most of us do when we're on the cusp of radical change. We like our well-worn ruts. We prefer our old familiar pain to unfamiliar anything.

"You are in touch with your pain, and that's beautiful," I added.

Natalia shot me a look that screamed, *You sadistic motherfucker.* Or at least, this was my interpretation. I pressed on: "By 'beautiful,' I mean these uncomfortable emotions are your truth, and your truth is the source of your new motivation to follow your heart—to stop ignoring your own desires. Accepting extreme painful feelings and responding to them is the only thing that pushes many of us toward necessary, life-affirming change."

Your Desires Have Value

"You say you can see clearly now," I said. "Can you give me an example of something you're seeing with clarity now and why it hurts?"

"My friend wanted to bring something for me to Jason's graduation party. She knows I've been going through a lot. So, she asks me over text, 'What's your favorite dessert?'"

"And?"

"It seems like a small thing, but you know what I started typing? Apple pie. I hate apple pie!"—she snorted—"so, I catch myself in the moment and realize here's my friend, wanting to do something just for me, and I'm on auto-pilot: I'm telling her Rob's favorite dessert! My default mode. Because I've been brainwashed. But now I actually notice the brainwashing. This is what I wanted to tell my friend: I want tiramisu. I love tiramisu! That's what I want! I don't want any crappy apple pie! I wanted to shout it, but then I felt like a toddler throwing a tantrum—all that I, I, I!"

"Natalia, there are no 'small' fucks. You're getting in tune with your own needs! This is huge! You're channeling your inner tiramisu-loving toddler. Radical Emotional Acceptance is not just about accepting our so-called 'negative' emotions, but also our positive emotions, desires, preferences, tastes, and passions. So much of what psychology defines as codependency is when you are not living your own preferences. Your desires have value. Look at how you light up with energy when you start to reclaim them."

Natalia nodded knowingly. "Other people could see what he was doing to me. Even my own son says, 'Dad sucks the life out of you. If you're staying with him because of me and Nathan, we'll be fine.' My own son said that to me, and it's still taken me this long to see." Natalia's voice now came out husky and hoarse, but with incredible force. "I can finally see I have a chance. There are people in my life who will back me up. But you know who didn't stand a chance at all?" I noticed her body begin to shake. She curled up tighter into her millipede ball and swiped at her tears with the backs of her hands. "Oh God, I feel like I'm talking to Rob! I have something so big, so fucking big. It's crushing my chest and I can't even get it out! It's just like being around him! I feel like I'm literally choking when I try to speak my deepest—"

Natalia rocked back and forth on the couch, fluttering her hands like her palms were on fire. I could sense she was approaching a deep truth. Something so consequential that, if she truly accepted it, there would be no turning back.

"You know who had zero chance? My own twin sister!"

The hairs stood up on the back of my neck. Natalia had never before mentioned they were twins.

"And you know I'm the big sister? I was born a minute ahead. I could have done something! I could have woken the fuck up, and I could have saved her! And now look at me: walking on eggshells in front of my husband, in front of my niece—her beautiful little girl. That's what's killing me the most about all this. That this little girl has traded one abusive household for another. That all she's known is her own mother and aunt acting like submissive, brainwashed, trapped women. Grown-ass women acting like shit scared little girls. That's all she's known. It's like this tight fucking bull's-eye drawn around our family tree and no one gets out alive. Oh god, oh god, I don't think I can—"

"Natalia." I looked directly into her eyes. "Are you ready to tell me about your sister? Are you ready to share why your niece is living with you?"

"Because my sister fucking hung herself, okay!"

She screamed it. When you've been suppressing your emotions for as long as Natalia, extreme anger is often the first emotion that comes to the surface.

"My sister fucking hung herself. There, I told you!" she repeated. She chewed the inside of her cheek now, toggling between rage and tears in a matter of seconds. "She killed herself nine years ago this week. Not that I'll ever forget the day, but, now that I'm seeing things for what they are, the timing is not lost on me. Now that I'm channeling my energy into moving on. I bought my truck this week. You know what today is?"

Tears filled my eyes as well. I very much wanted to know what today was.

"It's my liberation day. It should have been my sister's, too. More like this day nine years ago should have been her liberation day. It should have been the day she left him. Not the day she left this world."

Natalia pinched the bridge of her nose with her fingers. There was a part of her that was still guarding those fuck gates.

"But that bastard had everyone fooled. He was smooth," she finally shared. "The kind of husband who cooks only when you have houseguest over and makes them fancy cocktails and waits on them hand on foot. The kind of guy everyone gushes over: 'What an amazing man you have to help out like that, what a committed father—look at him doing the dishes! Aren't you a lucky lady!' Yadda, yadda." Natalia made a yapping motion with her free hand as her eyes narrowed. "But he didn't fool me. In many ways, my sister's husband was a bigger narcissist than Rob. But Jeremy was subtle about it. He played house, you know? He could act like he cared, but it was all a script. In front of everyone but his own family—he would turn it on like a 120-watt bulb. Everyone talked about his charisma. *Charisma.*" She spit the word out like an epithet. "I hate that fucking word."

"Natalia. I feel profound sorrow for your loss. I can't imagine the pain of losing a sibling, let alone a twin."

Natalia shrugged off my condolence. "He was always giving her these compliments," she snorted. "Compliments laced with cyanide. 'That dress flatters you, honey. It almost hides all the weight you've gained!' He was so much like our own mother. It was all about the show with him. Appearances. Surfaces. Funhouse mirrors. He would crank up the charm with strangers, but as soon as the company was gone and my sister was alone with him, it was passive-aggression, it was the silent treatment, it was—what is that word you use?—microaggressions. Just like our mother. He would chip away at my sister's self-worth in private while treating her like a queen when non-family members were around. Of course, no one else would back her up when she finally began sharing how he treated her. He carefully set it up that way. But it was all an act. A crazy-making act."

I leaned forward in my chair. Natalia had just described a covert narcissist, as opposed to an obvious narcissist like her husband. I felt immense compassion for Natalia as well as deep sadness for her sister's plight.

"What you just told me about your sister's husband is the definition of *gaslighting*.

And the way you describe not only your brother-in-law's behavior, but your mother's behavior, is covert passive-aggressive narcissism. Having grown up in the shadow of a covert narcissist, you know it all too well, and that's why it sounds like you were the only person who could see it in your sister's husband. Could your sister see his narcissism herself?"

"What do you think?" Natalia said jeeringly. I didn't take her tone personally. I could tell she was profoundly hurting. "Does someone who can accept their emotions hang themselves? My sister and I both fell for narcissists, like some sort of pre-ordained family script. She thought her feelings were the problem. She buried them so deep. She never learned that our feelings are our way out. And now it's too damn late. Almost a decade too late," Natalia howled.

Our Feelings Are Our Way Out

"Did you hear what you just said?" Natalia blinked. "*Our feelings are our way out.* I don't think that's something you could see so clearly—even a week ago. From what you're describing to me, you and your sister were raised not to expect unconditional love. How could you have saved your sister from her own nightmare nine years ago if, only a couple weeks ago, you couldn't save yourself?"

"Why do I always have to reach a breaking point before I do anything? My sister might be alive today." She loudly exhaled. "My niece would still have a mother," she intoned. She began to cry again. "And I didn't see it coming. And I didn't do a damn thing."

"Natalia, please listen carefully: Your breaking point was your son's graduation party. It sounds like an awful experience, but still, it was a party. Nothing more. But you'd already started practicing Radical Emotional Acceptance. You'd begun to acknowledge your feelings—even the incredibly painful and messy ones we label as negative—as valuable *emotional data*. You'd begun to accept your deeper feeling as appropriate responses to certain situations. If you hadn't first reached this level of acceptance, how could you possibly have started channeling your energy into leaving? If you hadn't figured out how to save yourself, how could you have saved your sister?"

"You're having a completely appropriate emotional response." I continued. "Your emotions are in your body, and your embodied feelings are your road map to a better life. Trauma traps us in a fugue state where we lose sight of who we really are—of our reality and self-worth."

True Love is Unconditioned

"Here's what I know," I said. "Emotional suppression allows codependent narcissistic relationships to grow. It's fuel for a terrible flame. You can't have the toxic relationship without the emotional suppression. No one would be able to stay with a narcissist for more than a month without starting to deny their emotions—not only the emotions we label as negative, but also our positive emotions—our joys, our desires, our preferences, and our tiramisu."

"I think of REA as a vaccine," I continued. "It protects us from getting swept up in toxic relationships, because it keeps us honest. Honest with ourselves. Many people have to reach a breaking point in their lives in order to make necessary change. With Radical Emotional Acceptance, you see you always have a choice."

"I feel deep sadness right now that this comes too late for your sister," I continued. "And yet I feel hopeful, because it's not too late for you. It's not too late for your niece or your sons, either. Accepting sadness makes room for hope and direction. REA takes practice, but it keeps us from needing to hit rock bottom again before we make change. It helps us make better choices so that we don't have to experience the same hell ever again. Acceptance allows us to move forward even when we can't forgive, even when the other party won't change their behavior. And it has nothing to do with the other person—with the abuser. It's something you do for yourself that also becomes a gift you can give your children."

"My sister left a note," Natalia said quietly. "More like a Post-it. You know what it said?

She let the question hang in the air.

"*Dear Jeremy, you win.* That's it. That's the last thing she ever said."

My heart broke for this woman. And for the twin sister I would never get to meet. She had so completely lost her sense of self, even her suicide note was about her husband.

"There's no winning with someone stuck in unrepentant covert narcissistic behavior," I said. "There's only one healthy way out, and it's to channel your energy into moving on. When I look at you, Natalia, I see someone who's been tested over and over. I also see someone who's self-worth is rising up and saying, I deserve better. I can do better. I will do better. And you never could have gotten to where you are today, at this exact moment—holding the keys to your own car and planning your exit strategy—if you'd denied your fucks. You couldn't go where you're going if you hadn't allowed yourself to feel the depths of your emotions. True love is unconditioned. It's either unconditional love or a perversion of love."

"That's what I feel for my children," Natalia said. "That's what I feel for my boys and my niece."

"So, if they deserve unconditional love, don't you?"

Natalia slowly uncoiled herself while we were speaking. The backs of her hands now rested lightly on her knees, her empty palms open to the ceiling.

"My love feels fierce today. It carries the weight of this terrible knowledge, but it also feels big as the sky.

Like as long as I'm honest with myself about what I'm truly feeling, I can be the sky to my children. I can shelter and protect. I'm not destroyed. I'm connecting the dots, and I feel stronger than I've felt in a long time. And that fierce love . . . I'm starting to feel it for myself. I'm starting to love myself unconditionally, in spite of everything that's happened."

"I'm happy for you for facing your reality—not arguing with it; not contesting it. For acknowledging what's really happening. And I'm impressed by your courage to share such a deep, painful truth about your sister. That's how you change. That's how you start to heal. And it's not about letting your husband off the hook. It's not about letting your brother-in-law off the hook, either. Unlike forgiveness, Radical Emotional Acceptance has nothing to do with the other person. You do it for yourself. "

"You know that song, 'Don't Worry, Be Happy'?" Natalia asked. "When my sister and I were kids, we thought it would be funny if the lyrics went, 'Don't Worry, Life's Crappy.' Emily and I,"—she stopped to blow her nose into a tissue—"Emily and I would even sing it that way. Of course, it would piss our mother off—Mrs. Perfect. When that song comes on the radio, I still sing it my way. I still sing it *our way*."

"And how does it make you feel? Singing *Don't Worry, Life's Crappy*?"

"It makes me feel like I've had the answers all along, but somewhere along the way I lost sight of myself. Of everything. If I'd only understood that it was okay to feel crappy, I could have stopped beating myself up a long time ago. I would have understood that that crappy feeling existed for a purpose. That crappy feeling was pointing me toward the emergency exit. And you know the wildest part? Right this second, I feel grateful. Despite everything that's happened, I feel grateful that I finally get it: my emotions are my way out."

The 5th Acceptance
Thank the Fuck
Your fucks are your friends.

Chapter 5

Thank the Fuck

Y*ou could say that I'm a dreamer*, and you'd be right: I was born the same year John Lennon was shot dead. I've long felt the most radical Beatle's spiritual juju pushing me forward in life—toward greater creativity, risk-taking, and self-discovery. Radical Emotional Acceptance is the most effective path I've found out of the Emotional Dark Ages. I've seen over and over again—not only in my therapeutic practice, but in my own life—how REA functions as a powerful catalyst for transformations both profound and subtle.

If, after reading this book, a giant dry eraser comes for your mind, just remember this one simple truth: My fucks serve a purpose.

What's the point of my suffering, my self-talk, the sour pit of fear in my small intestine? The purpose they serve is you. At some point or another, many of us tried to convince ourselves "I just don't give a fuck." To cover up our decades of stank, we spritzed ourselves with a no-fucks-given Febreze. But guess what? It didn't work.

If you've been trying The Acceptances on for size as you read along, you may have experienced a fascinating phenomenon: the more open you are to honoring your fucks, the easier your life becomes. It's that simple.

Through Radical Emotional Acceptance, you've learned to radically accept your emotional responses and use their valuable *emotional data* to make better life decisions. You have come to regard your painful emotions with respect, because they serve as valuable signposts that give us the motivation to make change. By feeling into your body and validating your emotions, whatever they may be, you can tap into your *sixth sense*. You may have even paused to appreciate your positive emotions, too, which give you insight into what you truly desire and value. This kind of specificity is what allows you to see with clarity when your relationships are not in alignment with your deepest values. By accepting your emotions without judgment, you will come to validate your basic human need for unconditional love. In short, you will come to radically accept yourself.

As a young boy in the West, I sometimes felt like a "show child"—a high-achieving but docile credit to my family name. There is a seed of truth in the American myth of the taciturn, emotionally uncommunicative cowboy. Throughout my childhood, I received the subtle and sometimes unsubtle message that certain emotions— sadness and anger in particular—were off limits. I used to think it was bad to raise my voice or to bite back like a German Shepard when its tail is yanked. I remember being scolded for looking like I was feeling sad, "Buck up" and "Stop moping around!"

It truly takes a village to emotionally suppress a child.

Now I celebrate all of life's rich emotions—even the most complicated ones, like jealousy or fear of success. Most people say they fear failure, but if you take a hardboiled look at human behavior, you might observe far more people shirking success. The currency of my childhood in a close-knit community was fitting in; not standing out. I feared "shining" in such a way that I lost friends. I feared being a tall poppy in a field of brilliant red.

All of my emotions are pointing me toward deep truths about myself and my relationships—toward a better way of living. And "all" is the operative word: everybody and their dog teaches you to practice gratitude for the things you like. It's easy to be thankful for good health, a loving relationship, or four wins in a row on the roulette wheel at the Bellagio. I'm not knocking gratitude for oxygen in our lungs or food on the table. People testify all the time to how a daily gratitude practice of meditation or journaling has changed their life for the better.

But do you know what's truly transformational? Finding gratitude for all the things you don't like. Practicing gratitude for difficult emotions, people, and situations is a lot harder than ecstatic journaling over that pot-o'-gold inheritance from your Great Aunt Marge. It's harder, but it's ultimately more rewarding. Finding value in emotions our brains label as "negative" orients us toward peace.

Here's the secret: If you're thankful for everything that happens to you, even in the midst of sorrow, you can always find your way back to a place of serenity. You are no longer in battle with reality. When you wage war, you're the one who suffers. Meanwhile, Reality is at the spa getting a hot stone massage. Reality can relax, because she knows she doesn't have to change a damn thing about herself.

Finding gratitude for our problems, finding gratitude for our discomforting emotions, and finding gratitude for our pain puts us back in our leather recliner at our own personal cinema. We get to settle in with our popcorn and enjoy our movie. We notice when we're trying to fast forward, or *emotionally bypass,* the hard stuff. We stay for the full ride; the tragedies and the triumphs.

Here's the magic: When we're able to creatively find gratitude for every aspect of our life journey, we're in touch with our own inner Yoda. When we radically accept our emotions surrounding how we should be treated by other people, our personal *agency* expands. We don't hesitate to stand up for ourself or to move on from toxic relationships.

Once you start to practice REA, you find yourself with a newfound superpower: you are no longer able to put up with other people's bullshit. Even better, you don't suffer your own bullshit. You start to realize all the times and places in your life when you've eaten shit, made excuses for yourself or others, self-sabotaged, or otherwise put up with disrespect from partners, family members, friends, bosses, asshats, or total pricks. You learn to speak softly, but carry a big stick. The magic in speaking your truth is that people are much more likely to listen closely to what you have to say.

Learning from Pain

We all start out with the assumption that pain is bad. But have you ever been around someone who was born without pain receptors? The rare condition is called congenital insensitivity to pain (CIPA); it effects about one in a million people. From birth, people who suffer from CIPA never feel pain in any part of their body when injured. Sound like a bottle of laudanum and feather bed in heaven?

Think again. The inability to feel pain is a massive extra dollop of life suffering. CIPA is unimaginably dangerous; in most cases, people with this tragic condition don't live beyond the age of 25. CIPA sufferers must constantly check for burns, bruises, cuts, and other unfelt injuries. If they live to see 25, they are usually disfigured by broken bones, burns, and other scarring. Imagine if the first time you touched a hot stove you didn't instantly draw back your hand? Now imagine that scenario happening over and over, perhaps for a couple decades. It's not pretty.

It is in this spirit I write, pain is good. It is our best teacher. Pain is a formidable taskmaster, for sure, but feeling pain, as long as we learn from it, is in our best interest. I spend hours playing with my two-year-old daughter, the youngest of my three girls, and she's constantly playing and hurting herself. Some days the sharp wood corners of our coffee table are her sagest teacher. Sometimes she will cry, but more often than not, she will laugh at the silliness of her tumbles. In the theater of life, children naturally love learning from cause and effect—what an academic might call "experiential learning" and what a parent calls "repercussions." This is how my baby girl is coming to navigate the world and trust herself.

Once you experience the REA of all your joys and sorrows, you will be amazed by what they have to teach you. You can celebrate the many ways your fucks guide you, instead of dismissing what you truly feel, playing Whack-A-Mole with your painful emotions, or telling yourself, "I just don't give a fuck." Finding gratitude for our emotional and physical pain—for all our hard-earned fucks—is the final Acceptance. I write *thank the fuck,* because I know accepting the validity of our truest feelings often requires a type of self-reinvention. The Five Acceptances facilitate a kind of self-transformation that is cause for celebration.

As Natalia courageously realized in the previous chapter, even our "small fucks" matter. They are our way out of the maze of suffering, and they lead us towards better self-understanding.

I experienced many powerful emotions while writing this book. As a doctor, I see many patients a day. I have three daughters 13 and under, and a baby boy on the way in October. Our due date is Halloween and my eight-year-old is sincerely worried she might have to miss trick-or-treating. She calls her new brother our "vampire baby."

Another great side effect of practicing REA? You find yourself laughing a hell of a lot more. Real, full-bodied laughter—not the nervous kind used to deflect uncomfortable emotions.

Truth be told, without practicing REA, I would have given up before I even started writing this book. This irony is not lost on me. Radically accepting the emotion of feeling overwhelmed—by the book, patients, paperwork, kids, baby, oh my!—allowed me to stay on course. Because I didn't fight my feelings of overwhelm, because I tried to learn from them, I was able to follow my heart through an insanely busy time amid a topsy-turvy global pandemic. I was able to put my time where my mouth is and to pursue a cherished dream—the book you are reading—in the midst of a maelstrom of feelings.

Through practicing REA, we're often able to get more out of life than we ever thought possible.

Which brings me to the final lesson of Radical Emotional Acceptance. We all have the need to experience unconditional love. I call it a need, because if it's not met, we experience mental, emotional, and bodily symptoms, and name-your-drug-of-choice addictions. Every mental health problem I have ever encountered stems, on some level, from not being loved unconditionally: by our parents, our friends, and, most importantly, ourselves.

Radical Emotional Acceptance is self-love. REA is the *how* of loving yourself: a field guide for validating your emotions and desires. And here's another big secret: giving yourself the experience of being loved unconditionally is a choice. We get to choose to only receive unconditional love in our relationships, and we get to choose to love ourselves unconditionally.

When we are aware of this noble truth, our eyes are open to reality. In this universe, there is an abundance of unconditional love for all of us. We just have to reach for it, dare I say—accept it.

Appendix
Glossary of Original Terms

Emotiaphobia – A fear of emotions. We are so irrationally scared of getting forever stuck in a fuck rut, we don't allow ourselves to feel discomforting emotions, not even for a second. We go to great lengths to deny, suppress, avoid, and skip over difficult emotions, turning our temporary pain into prolonged suffering.

Emotional Data – Fucks of all sizes provide precious information that can guide us towards self-understanding. Rather than treating our emotions like unwanted house guests, we can welcome them into our homes and hear what they have to tell us. Our emotions give voice to our true needs, values, and desires. By being receptive to their signals, we become better in touch with ourselves, and more open to connection with others. When a difficult emotion arises in our bodies, it is easy to feel like there must be something we need to *do*. We want specific results; namely, for the emotion to go away. REA is not a new, more sophisticated technique for getting fucks to stop. Problem-solving our emotions, before we've even heard them out, doesn't work. They just yell louder. Instead, we can take the time to listen to their wisdom with openness and curiosity.

Fuck Blocking – In our misguided attempt to spare ourselves from feeling, we create distance between ourselves and our truth. We reach for shiny, quick-acting fuck-denying mechanisms, or wall ourselves off from our fucks with mile-high shield emotions. We try to game the system to skip over our root emotions, but the system cannot be rigged. The only way out is through—by feeling our fucks fully. The key is not to shame ourselves for our noble attempts to bypass pain, but simply notice when we are engaging in fuck-blocking behavior.

Fuck-Denying Mechanism – These are both obvious and not so obvious behaviors we use to avoid our fucks, or allow ourselves a break from the intensity of a feeling. Think about the last thing you reached for in a moment of unease. Did you roll a spliff after a hard week at the office, or make a dad joke during an awkward conversation? Aside from actively hurting ourselves and others, fuck-denying mechanisms in themselves are not unhealthy. We all have them. But once we recognize what we tend to cling to, as an easy way to stave off our fucks, we will feel much more in the driver's seat of our days. We may even find we don't need as many fuck-denying mechanisms, because we are open to processing our fucks instead.

Fuck Gates – The catch 22 of fucks: although we try hard to deny our emotions, we desperately want to feel them in full. The body is designed to release tension. Fuck Gates are an inflection point, like levees bursting after a Category 5 hurricane. After so much pernicious fuck-blocking, there is a powerful release that comes from putting down our defenses and allowing our fucks to flow freely. Our body expels energy in countless ways—through a guttural scream, a series of yawns, or one long, mournful sigh. At first, the process may feel unfamiliar, even frightening, but once we give ourselves permission to let the Fuck Gates open, we can experience the relief on the other side.

Radical Emotional Acceptance – REA is the practice of accepting each and every emotion, as they come, in real time. If you think of emotions as colors in the rainbow, you cannot choose to see only blue, or ignore red entirely. Emotions are a package deal. Once we acknowledge the emotions in our bodies, rather than deny or ignore their calls, we can learn from the emotional data they offer. We can treat them with the reverence they deserve, because they are our wisest teachers. We can become curious and ask our dear emotions—what say you?—rather than blaming them for ruining an otherwise good day, or making a painful situation even worse. Our emotions are signposts for what we truly give a fuck about in this world, and guide us towards a life of integrity.

Root Emotions – These are the core, raw emotions in our heart of hearts. They are at the root of all of our behaviors, thoughts, and feelings. While we humans make things complicated by intellectualizing and rationalizing, our root emotions are simple. In fact, once we turn off our overly analytic prefrontal cortex, and ask ourselves—*what are we really feeling?*—we can answer truthfully. Everything becomes clear as day. Just think about a time when you were hurting, and a friend who knows you really well looked you straight in the eyes, and you couldn't help but start tearing up. The root emotions are our deep truths: the fear, pain, terror, grief, loneliness, joy, and love. They connect us to ourselves and to others. But often, we are scared of our root emotions. Instead, we swaddle ourselves in shield emotions.

Shield Emotions – Shield emotions exist on the surface—like the tip of the proverbial Anger Iceberg—to protect ourselves from more vulnerable Root Emotions underneath. Even our emotions have their own built in Fuck-Denying Mechanism! Sometimes called secondary emotions, shield emotions are reactive and easy to access: anger, jealousy, blame, resentment, annoyance, agitation, disappointment, numbness, detachment, or hysterical elation. These quick-to-the-trigger emotions are sneaky, because they can make us feel like we are experiencing the full range of our emotions, when in reality, we're still skimming the surface. Generally, shield emotions create distance—between our minds and our hearts, between ourselves and others.

Okay, repeat after me:

We all have emotional reactions (hereby called Fucks). Because of **Emotiaphobia,** we use our go-to **Fuck-Denying Mechanism** to avoid feeling our Fucks. But even if we deny their existence, our Fucks get stored in our bodies. To avoid feeling our most vulnerable **Root Emotions,** we cling to surface-level **Shield Emotions.** Through **Radical Emotional Acceptance,** we come to welcome our fucks and appreciate the **Emotional Data** they provide. In doing so, we can live with ease and make decisions that are in line with our authentic selves.

Acknowledgments

I would like to start by radically emotionally accepting the pure gratitude I feel for every step of this journey and the team who helped make this book possible. For me, gratitude is an emotion that is both joyful and deeply humbling. It reminds us just how much we need each other and how good it feels to have that need met.

I would have to write another book to thank every person who has touched my life and filled me with gratitude. I feel privileged to have chosen a profession that puts me in touch with the depths of human sorrows and joys.

To my wife, Aya. I experience your unconditional love for me every day in your own unique love language. Thank you for putting up with all the stolen hours it took to create this slender book. Wherever I may wander in life, there you are.

Besides the wonderful folks I get to serve as patients, my own children are my greatest teachers. Daddy wants nothing more than to give you the true experience of unconditional love. Thank you for letting me know when I'm failing.

Words alone cannot express my gratitude for being raised in my family. My mother, who has a wicked sense of humor, recently quoted Nora Ephron to me: "A successful parent is one who raises a child so that they can pay for their own psychoanalysis." The unconditional love I received, in the midst of our trials, was the incubator that created this psychiatrist.

To my own therapists: you know who you are. HIPPA patient privacy rules prevent us (rightfully so) from naming each other, but I'd like to make an important point: healing is a lifelong process, and therapists have a lot in common with Russian nesting dolls. How, you might ask? Well, inside every therapist who gives a fuck about you is *their* therapists who gave a fuck about them. I feel deep gratitude for carrying your insights within me and for the ability to apply them toward my life and practice.

I've been fortunate to stand on the backs of giants. From my professors in medical school and attending psychiatrists in residency and fellowship, to the authors and thought leaders who have generously taken me under their wing over the years—thank you. I cherish what you have taught me and would need many more pages to name you all. I believe teaching is the noblest of professions: I can only hope you feel joy in seeing the seeds you planted grow into the synthesis that is Radical Emotional Acceptance.

Remember the dance scene in the Preston, Idaho, high school auditorium in *Napoleon Dynamite*? Napoleon needed his friend Pedro to teach him to follow his heart, be bold, and make his wildest dreams come true. To my friend Mary: Thank you for being my Pedro and teaching me never to settle.

To the team at Kevin Anderson & Associates for their editorial guidance and help in finding this book such a great home at Skyhorse Publishing—with whom it's been a pleasure to collaborate.

Finally, I will forever be endlessly grateful to those who helped with the production and development. Effectively communicating these precious ideas—to give them life and make them applicable for the reader—has been a deeply rewarding experience I enjoyed with you very much.

Give a Fuck, Actually existed in my mind for years before ever making its way onto the page. And yet, only after practicing REA, was I ready to begin. I had to reach a point of Radical Emotional Acceptance of *everything*: my blind spots, limitations, feelings of complete overwhelm, and, last but hardly least, accepting my own strengths and talents. I grew up in a society that valued not standing out—fuck those tall poppies—and this has made slapping my name on a book a daunting prospect. But this book is not about me. It's about helping you, the reader, with your emotional journey as an embodied being in this world.

Additional Resources

*A selection of some of the most influential books in my
conceptualization of REA:*

Barrett, Lisa Feldman. *How Emotions Are Made: The Secret
Life of the Brain.* Houghton Mifflin Harcourt, 2017.

Baum, Brent. *The Healing Dimensions: Resolving Trauma in
Body, Mind and Spirit.* First Edition, Healing Dimensions,
1997.

Benson, Kyle. "The Anger Iceberg." The Gottman
Institute, 8 November 2016. https://www.gottman.
com/blog/the-anger-iceberg/.

Ben-Shahar, Tal. *The Pursuit of Perfect: How to Stop Chasing
Perfection and Start Living a Richer, Happier Life.* 1st ed.,
McGraw-Hill Education, 2009.

Brach, Tara. *Radical Acceptance: Embracing Your Life With
the Heart of a Buddha.* Reprint, Bantam, 2004.

Brach, Tara. *Radical Compassion: Learning to Love Yourself and Your World With the Practice of RAIN.* Viking, 2019.

Brown, Brené. *The Gifts of Imperfection: Let Go of Who You Think You're Supposed to Be and Embrace Who You Are.* 1st ed., Hazelden Publishing, 2010.

Caligor, Eve, et al. *Psychodynamic Therapy for Personality Pathology: Treating Self and Interpersonal Functioning.* 1st ed., Amer Psychiatric Pub Inc, 2018.

Johnson, Sue. *Hold Me Tight: Seven Conversations for a Lifetime of Love.* 1st ed., Little, Brown Spark, 2008.

Elkrief, Noah. *A Guide to The Present Moment.* Noah Elkrief, 2012.

Frankl, Viktor, et al. *Man's Search for Meaning.* 1st ed., Beacon Press, 2006.

Hayes, Steven, and Spencer Smith. *Get Out of Your Mind and Into Your Life: The New Acceptance and Commitment Therapy (A New Harbinger Self-Help Workbook).* 1st ed., New Harbinger Publications, 2005.

Hendricks, Gay. *The Big Leap: Conquer Your Hidden Fear and Take Life to the Next Level.* 1st ed., HarperOne, 2010.

Hersh, Richard, et al. *Fundamentals of Transference-Focused Pscyhotherapy.* New York-United States, Springer Publishing, 2017.

Gottman, John. *The Science of Trust: Emotional Attunement for Couples.* W. W. Norton, 2011.

Katie, Byron, and Stephen Mitchell. *Loving What Is: Four Questions That Can Change Your Life.* Reprint, Three Rivers Press, 2003.

Kreisman, Jerold, and Hal Straus. *I Hate You—Don't Leave Me: Understanding the Borderline Personality*. Revised, Updated, TarcherPerigee, 2010.

Levine, Amir, and Rachel Heller. *Attached: The New Science of Adult Attachment and How It Can Help You Find - and Keep - Love*. Illustrated, TarcherPerigee, 2012.

LeVine, Peg. *Classic Morita Therapy*. Abingdon-United Kingdom, United Kingdom, Taylor & Francis, 2017.

Linehan, Marsha. *DBT Skills Training Manual, Second Edition*. Second Edition, Available separately: *DBT Skills Training Handouts and Worksheets*, Second, The Guilford Press, 2014.

Mirza, Debbie. "The Covert Passive-Aggressive Narcissist: Recognizing the Traits and Finding Healing After Hidden Emotional and Psychological Abuse." Debbie Mirza Coaching, 2017.

Ruiz, Don Miguel, Don Jose Ruiz, et al. *The Fifth Agreement: A Practical Guide to Self-Mastery (Toltec Wisdom)*. Amber-Allen Publishing, 2011.

Ruiz, Don Miguel, Jill Eikenberry, et al. *The Mastery of Love: A Practical Guide to the Art of Relationships*. Abridged edition, Amber-Allen Publishing, 2002.

Ruiz, Miguel. *The Four Agreements*. Amber-Allen Pub., 1997.

Schwartz, Richard, and Martha Sweezy. *Internal Family Systems Therapy, Second Edition*. Second, The Guilford Press, 2019.

Smith, Watt Tiffany. *Schadenfreude: The Joy of Another's Misfortune*. Little, Brown Spark, 2018.

Stout, Martha. *The Sociopath Next Door.* 1st ed., Harmony, 2006.

Watts, Alan, and Chopra Deepak Md. *The Wisdom of Insecurity: A Message for an Age of Anxiety.* 2nd ed., Vintage Books, 2011.

Yalom, Irvin. *The Gift of Therapy: An Open Letter to a New Generation of Therapists and Their Patients* (Covers May Vary). 1st ed., Harper Perennial, 2017.

Index